The Norfolk Nightmare

David Thurlow, who was born in Wisbech, Cambs., has spent most of his working life as a reporter for national papers in East Anglia, covering many of the crimes in this book. Under his own name and the pseudonym Jonathan Macgowan, he has written thirteen crime thrillers. He now works for *The Times*.

By the same author

The Essex Triangle

The Norfolk Nightmare

A Chronicle of Murders and Disappearances

David Thurlow

ROBERT HALE · LONDON

ISBN 0 7090 4514 X

Robert Hale Limited
Clerkenwell House
Clerkenwell Green
London EC1R 0HT

Photoset in North Wales by
Derek Doyle & Associates, Mold, Clwyd.
Printed in Great Britain by
St Edmundsbury Press, Bury St Edmunds, Suffolk.
and bound by WBC Bookbinders Ltd, Bridgend, Glamorgan.

Contents

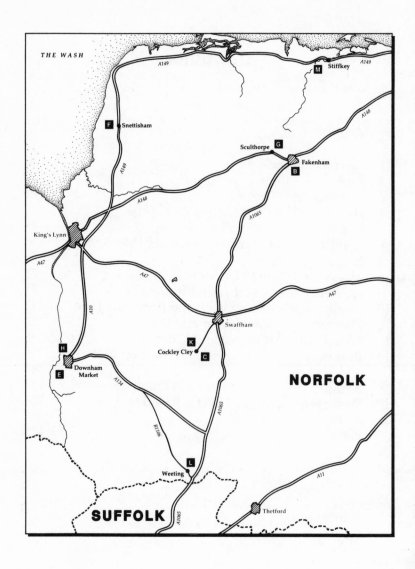

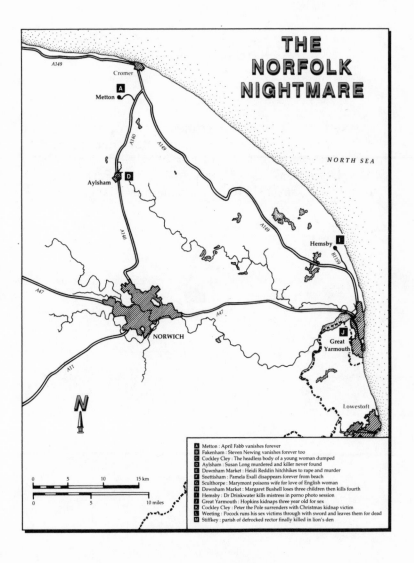

THE NORFOLK NIGHTMARE

A149

Cromer

A - Metton

A140

A149

Aylsham - D

A140

NORTH SEA

A149

Hemsby - I

B1159

A47

A47

NORWICH

A11

Great Yarmouth - J

N

Lowestoft

0	5	10	15 km
0	5		10 miles

A Metton : April Fabb vanishes forever
B Fakenham : Steven Newing vanishes forever too
C Cockley Cley : The headless body of a young woman dumped
D Aylsham : Susan Long murdered and killer never found
E Downham Market : Heidi Reddin hitchhikes to rape and murder
F Snettisham : Pamela Exall disappears forever from beach
G Sculthorpe : Marymont poisons wife for love of English woman
H Downham Market : Margaret Bushell loses three children then kills fourth
I Hemsby : Dr Drinkwater kills mistress in porno photo session
J Great Yarmouth : Hopkins kidnaps three year old for sex
K Cockley Cley : Peter the Pole surrenders with Christmas kidnap victim
L Weeting : Pocock runs his sex victims through with sword and leaves them for dead
M Stiffkey : parish of defrocked rector finally killed in lion's den

Acknowledgements

I covered many of these crimes as a reporter but my thanks go to Maureen Huggins for her unrivalled knowledge of the cases and her help, and also to Tony Scase, Denis Cassidy, Don Leigh, Brian Park, and my colleagues in *The Times* library for their assistance.

1

Norfolk

Introduction

Norfolk is a huge county of over a million acres with large areas unpopulated, with forests, woodlands and moorlands, neolithic caves and the ghosts that are associated with them, rivers and ponds and long sweeping roads filling the flat land. Towns and villages are isolated and the population is sparse with most people living in Norwich or the few towns. Around this vast piece of East Anglia are over 90 miles of coastline on the North Sea.

What more attractive place could there be to the man who wants to snatch a girl from the roadside, to a killer who wants to dump the body in the lonely moonlight when the deer and foxes pad silently through the gorse and bracken or on a night when the fog swirls with the rain and the sky hangs like lead above them with shivering winds, or to the child molester who wants to fulfil his perverted desires and then dispose of the victim?

There are few places with the ingredients that Norfolk can provide for the disposal of evil. This is a county where the people in the countryside go to their homes early for they have to be up early. Cars go by but they are heard, not seen. Their make and numbers are not recorded.

This book is about those people who have snatched and dumped in the county, some to be caught, others to vanish with their victims who have never been found either. A county like Norfolk brings criminals from far away. It may not have the motorways that are used by criminals all over Britain for access and escape. But the fact that the roads are nothing special has its compensation with little traffic, particularly on the A roads at night. You can still drive for miles through the forests without seeing many vehicles. Police cars are out and about but they have to patrol enormous tracts of countryside. There are side roads into the woods and trees, tracks that can be seen in the daylight and used at night.

It is certain that the bodies that have been found are but a fraction of those hidden, probably by those who have taken every precaution not to have them found and have not panicked in the closing moments of disposal when nerves fail and fear and guilt takes over.

So what is it that brings the wicked to the area, that stirs the locals to use it as well?

Norfolk is a bulge that runs from the Wash at the top on the Lincolnshire border down to Great Yarmouth, still a favourite seaside resort, and just beyond in the south. At the top on the coast is Hunstanton, and then inland, before you hit Cromer, you have Sandringham where the royals spend Christmas, and Burnham Market where Nelson was born. South on the coast are Mundesley, Blakeney bird sanctuary and then the fishing ports and container terminals.

If a killer wants to throw a body into the sea there is plenty of it. If he wants to make sure that it does not come back he needs to study charts and tides. One mystery involves a girl student who went for a late night, last night of holiday walk along the beach on the Wash and has never been seen since.

But the sea for murder is always a risky business. Inland is so much better in a county where there are 750 medieval churches, hundreds of Roman and prehistoric sites, over 100 disused villages and 700 that are lived in, providing plenty of opportunities for hiding anything, even before you move on to the acres where only animals live, like the great expanse of Thetford Forest which seems enormous by British standards.

The television comedy *Dad's Army* was filmed in it. For

years it has included the Stanford Battle Area, one of the Army's main training grounds, taken over in the Second World War when the villagers moved out. Some still go back once a year to their shattered, shell-blasted old homes for services in roofless churches. The Army shares the land with the Forestry Commission. It is a mixture of woodland, heathland, streams and rivers – the perfect cover for crime.

The main road from London, the A11 that goes to Norwich and then becomes the A47 on to Great Yarmouth to the east and to King's Lynn and the Midlands to the north, dissects the forest, running from Barton Mills in Suffolk up to Thetford and on to Attleborough and Norwich. The body of a toddler was found in a man-made relief river on the border, hurled in in the dark by a man who barely deserves the name of human. She was alive when he threw her in to drown in the dank, cold water on a moonless night.

The A47 north to King's Lynn runs parallel with the coast and is an outer boundary for the sweeping woodland in the heart of the county. The A1065, which runs from Brandon on the Suffolk–Norfolk border, makes the third side of the triangle formed by the A11 and A47. The A1065 is favoured by holidaymakers going to the coast around Wells and Cromer and Sheringham and cuts a swathe through Swaffham Forest where there are Grimes Graves, the neolithic flintmines. The road is straight and fast with a few bends to slow the motorist down.

What better road could there be on which to travel to dispose of the headless body of a young woman who was an unwanted lover, or the limpet wife who had to be despatched in a ruthless manner and then dumped, trussed and bound in a parcel and left in undergrowth just off the road with very long odds against it being found. In fact the body was found, but no one knows who she was for the killer made certain that the nightie which he left on was one of tens of thousands sold by a chain store and that the wrapping and string were too common to be traced.

Not far away, just off another major artery road of the county, the A10 from London to Cambridge and Ely and then into Norfolk, just past Littleport along the banks of the Ouse, to King's Lynn, the body of a young girl was tossed into a deep ditch by a man who was eventually traced but only after the body had been there for some weeks.

Going north-east there is Downham Market on the A10, a pleasant market town where early on a Boxing Day morning a mother suffocated her young son, aged seven. This did not involve snatching or dumping but it was equally bizarre because of what had happened to three other of her children in the space of fourteen months many years before.

North-east is the town of Fakenham. It was there in 1969 that an 11-year-old boy walked out of his home to go to see a friend and vanished off the face of the earth. Also never seen since was a 13-year-old girl in a village not too far away, just outside Cromer, who went to deliver a birthday present to her sister's husband in the next village one Easter and disappeared. One moment she was riding her cycle along a country lane with people about, the next she had gone and her cycle was tossed over a high bank into a field. She was a pretty girl, fair haired and rosy cheeked from a loving family. It is a cliché but she, like the boy, vanished into thin air and neither have ever been seen or heard of since.

Just outside Fakenham is a huge USAF air base and it was there that a master sergeant poisoned his wife so that he could marry his English love who lived in Berkshire. His trial in the old film studios at Elstree where many court room dramas had been filmed was more dramatic than any fiction.

Not far from Fakenham and going towards Norwich is Aylsham, a market town on the edge of the Broads. A girl from the town caught the last bus home from Norwich after a night out with her boy friend. It was to be the last time she was to travel on the bus because she had bought herself a car and was to begin using it the next day. But she never did because on her walk home from the market place in Aylsham she was picked up and her battered body found in a lover's lane the next morning. Her killer has never been traced and nor has a mystery man seen running up to the bus just before it left Norwich that night. Whoever killed her had local knowledge.

Two who chose Norfolk for its hiding places were Pete the Pole and a plumber who had a sword to abduct and sexually attack two young teenagers he met in Cambridgeshire. He chose a wood in Norfolk to run them through with his sword and leave them for dead because he wanted no one to give evidence against him. Only the girls' courage kept them alive with horrific wounds so that he was caught. Pete the Pole took his victim, a girl he trapped just minutes into Christmas Day, eventually to Norfolk as he raped her time and time again before deciding that he would kill himself and her by driving head on into an oncoming car at high speed. He did, but the only fatal casualty was a baby in the other car.

More recently there was a woman from south London who was due to go to a funeral but who was murdered and her body brought to the Suffolk–Norfolk border where it was left beside a track. The post mortem was carried out in Great Yarmouth. She had no connections with East Anglia and the only reason she was brought there at the end of her life was because it was the best dumping ground. No one knows who killed her or why.

There are bizarre cases, too, domestic but strange. A doctor injected his lover with a lethal cocktail of relaxing drugs to take erotic pictures, but killed her. That happened in a sleepy seaside village. And there are bizarre characters like Harold Davidson, the rector of Stiffkey, long dead but not forgotten. To say that they are bizarre is not to criticize them because Norfolk people are headstrong, do not like foreigners much and are very independent.

Someone like a former high sheriff is typical of the Norfolk character. He had all his silverware stolen after his daughter's coming-out party. It was a grand affair with a leading orchestra from London and many guests at his stately home in the north of the county. He called in the

police but after a while he was not happy with the
progress that they were making in catching the thieves,
and decided to make his own investigations. He reasoned
that it could not have been one of the guests nor the band:
he knew none of them would behave in such an appalling
way to their host. He therefore suspected the catering
staff, and the only person whose name he knew was that
of the man who made the crêpes Suzette. He went to see
him and discovered, to his amazement, that not only was
he the thief but that he was in league with a professional
criminal. Eventually the sheriff recovered his silverware,
giving the thieves a start before ringing the police (who
were not best pleased by the sheriff's activities), and later
the two men appeared in the old-fashioned Assize court in
Norwich Castle.

The sheriff was quite different to the rector of Stiffkey
but in the same mould of person – determined,
single-minded. Davidson was defrocked in Norwich
Cathedral for immorality, a charge which he denied for
the rest of his days until he was killed by a lion called
Freddie in its cage on Skegness seafront. The rectory in the
tiny village of Stiffkey rang with the laughter of some of
the girls he tried to save and whom he occasionally
brought down to the countryside on Sundays in the
twenties. On other occasions the fields did too when the
girls tired of rectory life and looked to see what the locals
were doing. He adds some relief to the evil that has been
done.

It is true that there are killers to be found everywhere,
but this is an area of natural hiding places and lonely lanes
where people can vanish – an area that attracts those from
afar and makes the county different.

2

Fabb

The Missing Six Minutes

Two days after Easter, 1969, April Fabb, a few days short
of her fourteenth birthday, vanished off the face of the
earth and has not been seen since. It is a bald, terrifyingly
simple statement of fact. It happened in a matter of a few
minutes, possibly as long as nine, possibly as short as six,
but one moment she was cycling along a Norfolk country
lane and the next she was gone. For good. For ever.

8 April, 1969 was a lovely day, a day when parts of the
Norfolk countryside and coastal villages take on a stillness
and quiet of a Dutch painting in the light which is peculiar
to that part of the county. There is a stillness in the
sunshine and the greys and whites seem to find a
crispness they do not normally have. The village of
Metton, little more than a hamlet of fifty-seven people and
just inland from Cromer, was touched by that light that
morning, and in No. 3 of the council houses everyone but
April, who was on school holidays from Form 3A at
Cromer secondary modern school, got up.

She had a lie-in with her cairn terrier Trudy while her
father Ernest, a builder's labourer, her mother Olive, who
cleaned at St Andrew's Church rectory opposite their
home, and elder sister Diane, a shorthand typist, prepared
for work. Her mother was the last to leave at 9.20 a.m.
April, whose birthday was just fourteen days later, lay in
bed, surrounded by pictures plastered all over the wall of

15

her favourite popstar, Andy Fairweather Lowe. She was no doubt thinking about him and about her shopping expedition with a schoolfriend to Norwich about 30 miles away the next day.

April was a rosy-cheeked Norfolk girl, born in the house where she lived, with long fair hair and looking a couple of years older than her age. She had no boy friends and was shy and timid, warm and pleasant, a thoroughly nice girl from a thoroughly nice family. They lived a happy life in a backwater and loved it.

By the time Mrs Fabb came home from the rectory at 10.00 a.m. to collect some dusters she had forgotten, April was up, dressed in brown slacks and a green sweater. During the two hours until midday when Mrs Fabb came home from work, April took Trudy out for a good walk. She arrived home just after her mother.

Forty minutes later, a friend of the family who was also the mother of April's school friend called to bring a packet of cigarettes April had asked her to buy as a birthday present for the husband of another sister, Pam, and also to tell April the shopping trip was off because her daughter was ill.

After she left April sat on the sofa with tears in her eyes, tears of disappointment that made her mother suggest she ring another friend to see whether she would go. April went out, clambered on her blue and white bike and rode down to the phone box. Minutes later she was home to say the girl would go with her on Saturday.

A much happier girl then asked her mother what she could do in the afternoon. Mrs Fabb suggested that she rode over to Pam's house at Roughton, 2 miles away, to give Bernard his birthday present. The packet of ten cigarettes was to substitute the packet of sweets April had bought but eaten herself. She loved sweets. Her mother said that she had a blue handkerchief that April could take with the cigarettes.

After having something to eat April went upstairs and changed. She put on a red divided skirt to go with the green jumper, white bobby socks – which she normally did not wear, not even for school, because she thought she was too old for them – and her slip-on Scholl sandals. Just after 1.35 p.m. she kissed her mother goodbye as she left the house for the last time, got on her bike and set off for her sister's home, just a few minutes ride away down country lanes. In her bedroom she left her watch and money.

She travelled only 200 yards before she stopped. Two girls, Christine and Maureen, both aged twelve were playing with a donkey called Judy in a field. April knew them both and, propping her cycle – with the cigarettes wrapped in the hankie in her saddle-bag – joined them, walking them and Judy round the field. After a while she said that she must go on to Pam's.

At 2.06 p.m., 200 yards further on down the lane, the 5 feet 4 inches tall fair-haired girl was seen by a tractor driver who knew her as she rode by. That was the last time she was seen alive by anyone prepared to come forward.

At 2.15 p.m., nine minutes after the last positive sighting, at a time checked and rechecked by detectives, her cycle was seen in Three Cornered Field by three men working on an ordnance survey. The spot where the cycle was seen was 600 yards from her home and about 200 yards from where the tractor driver saw her just before Pill Box crossroads. The field was 150 yards past the crossroads and in view of the field where the two 12-year-old girls were playing with the donkey. To be in the spot where it was seen the cycle had to cross an 8-foot bank. It was obvious when it was found later that it had been thrown over the bank into the field. The bell had been dented and the way it lay showed what had happened.

No one knew April had, by that time, just in a few minutes – less than 500 seconds – gone. As far as her mother was concerned she was on her way to Pam's house.

At about 3.30 p.m. a local man spotted and retrieved the cycle and, concerned that it may have been stolen and dumped by the thief, handed it in to the village policeman at Roughton. In the saddle-bag was the birthday present and five pence halfpenny.

When her father and sister came home for tea after their day's work her mother told them that April must be having tea with Pam and she wished that April had told her before she left that she was going to stay. By 7.00 p.m. Mrs Fabb was getting worried but her husband told her that Bernard, his son-in-law, would be bringing April home and she should not worry. But she did. Like any mother she was anxious because it was not like her daughter. She was not a girl who stayed out without saying that she was going to. She might have stopped and chatted with her eldest sister without noticing the time but it would not have been for this long. April would have become anxious herself that her mother might be worrying about her, wondering why she was so long.

At 8.30 p.m. Mrs Fabb could not stand it any longer and got on her own cycle and rode over to Pam's house. It did not take long and once there she learnt the heart-stopping, the stomach-churning, the mouth-drying fact that April had never been there.

Where on earth was she? Bernard, her son-in-law, drove her back. She and her husband searched the small house, knowing that she was not there but hoping for some small hint that she had been back. But her watch and her money were in the same place as they had been, her slacks neatly folded on her bed.

Mr Fabb went across the road to the rectory to ring the police. They and the Fabbs and other villagers carried out the only search they could until daylight, checking every possible address where April could be: friends, the two girls with whom she had played with the donkey in Harrison's Field, school friends, the girl with whom she was going to Norwich, anybody. There was no trace of her. No one had seen her, no one had heard from her.

At 4.00 a.m. on 9 April Detective Chief Superintendent Reg Lester, who was then head of Norfolk CID and now in retirement still keeps an active interest in the case, was rung at home. He knew he was facing two obvious facts: she had either run away or she had been abducted.

The full rigour of a countryside search for clues started just after dawn on another lovely day. Dozens of policemen initially confined it to within 2 miles of April's home. Tracker dogs were brought in and a helicopter swept over the area.

The cycle that the local machine operator had found in the field was quickly matched with April and minutely examined. It was clear that it had been thrown by someone strong into the field – where, apart from the indentation of the cycle, the soil was not disturbed – because of the distance covered, a matter of 6 feet after going over the bank.

The police immediately asked the local press – and soon the nationals, and television – to use a photograph of April asking 'Have you seen this girl?' Posters went up in railway and bus stations and public places. The face that the public saw was that of a schoolgirl, a Norfolk girl with clear eyes and hair parted, in her school uniform. As the Fabbs waited anxiously at home, as the police hunted, the publicity brought results. By that evening they had two sightings: the driver and guard of the 3.58 p.m. Cromer to North Walsham train on the Tuesday afternoon said they had seen a girl resembling April board the train. Another person said they had seen a girl similar to April on the platform at North Walsham at 6.15 p.m. the same day.

Then, as the story became national property (and has remained ever since) a girl like April was seen on the 10.15 a.m. Norwich to London Eastern Counties coach, arriving at Victoria at 3.55 p.m. The driver remembered her because she was a shilling (5p) short of her fare.

The girl who was seen on North Walsham station platform later came forward.

The girl seen on the train, the girl seen on the coach, never did. Who they were and whether they were April remains a piece in the mystery that has never been solved.

What the police had to go on was this: the certainty of her parents that she would never go off on her own, that she had been seen by a man on his tractor, a man in a Land Rover and the surveyors, all before her cycle was found in the field. It was a narrow lane by the field where two cars would have difficulty in passing without stopping and then easing past.

Then there was a battered mini van with two youths in it that had been seen in Metton minutes before April disappeared. That was quickly eliminated when the boys came forward. They had seen nothing but two groups of schoolboys, car spotting to pass the time during their holiday, had compiled a list of over 400 cars that had been driving through the lanes around Roughton over Tuesday and Wednesday. It took weeks to track down the licence holders of the numbers that the boys had written down correctly. They had even logged the numbers of some of the reporters from far afield who had been following the trail to interview Pam and Bernard in Roughton.

There was a possibility that April had gone to see her hero Andy Fairweather Lowe, but that had not happened. She might also have tried to go to Australia to be with her male cousin, aged twenty-one, who had left the day April vanished. She made no secret of her envy, not the passionate kind but the 'I wish I was going too' type. Another blank. Perhaps she had gone to a concert of her favourite pop group, Amen Corner? But no, they were appearing in Belgium.

In those early days, that left just one more avenue to explore: the man who had found the cycle and retrieved it. Why had he done it in a county where the bike was an extremely common means of transport in those days and bikes could be seen leaning against gates, banks, trees or in fields while their owners worked. Why pick on this one lying in a field? The man who had found it was questioned closely. He told them that he had taken his mother into Cromer to the hospital to keep an appointment. While she went in, having reached the hospital at 2.15 p.m., the time April's cycle was first spotted, he took his young son to the boating lake, picked his mother up at 2.40 p.m. and took an unusual route home via Metton so that he could pick up some shoes his mother had left in a cobbler's for repair in Attleborough.

As they drove through the country lanes his mother, almost sixty, spotted the cycle lying in the field. Because it was a child's cycle and it seemed in a strange position their curiosity was aroused. How had it got there? It was because it was so odd that a child's bike should be in a field with no footprints around it that the man stopped at the gate, went and retrieved it and took it to the policeman at Roughton. The next morning, once the hue and cry for April began and of which he was part, the policeman recognized that it was hers.

The man who found it had done a good deed, he thought. But the police had been told by a witness who knew him that he had been approaching Metton at 2.00 p.m. It put the Good Samaritan in a terrible position for he became a key suspect. Police checked his account thoroughly but did not find the clincher to prove that he was right in everything he said until they went to the television hire shop where he had called with his son to pay his mother's rental. They operated a cash till system where the assistant wrote the name of each customer who made a payment and then wound the till on to the next one. By questioning those who paid just before or just after the Samaritan the police were able to pinpoint the exact time he went into the shop.

He was cleared from the inquiry. He knew that police had to check every possible lead but, as he said afterwards, even if he saw a battleship in a field he would not bother to report it.

As the week wore on April's disappearance became the main talking point in Norfolk. It was also a national event. Some children disappear and make local news, even reaching national level for a time, but then going from the headlines, a tragedy to the family but no longer to be shared by the nation. Just why that is so no one can explain logically. But sometimes, as in the case of April Fabb, the public sympathy, the manner of disappearance, the character of the girl, the behaviour of her parents, the dignity of those involved, the patience and hard work of the police, spark off something that becomes part of the national story. In April's case it happened and, ever since, every time a child of like age or similar manner of disappearance occurs, her name is mentioned. As the years go by and anniversaries come and go, her parents and family are interviewed, the same pictures come out,

the same feeling touches the hearts of those who read it or
see it on television and their hope, shared with police and
the girl's family, are that she can be found, that an
explanation can be discovered which could end the
torment of Mr and Mrs Fabb.

By Saturday, 12 April, when there had been no real clue
or lead to follow, Chief Superintendent Lester held a
conference of his officers in the incident room at Cromer.
Over thirty sat down to see a new aspect of the shy girl
they were seeking. It was a film, an amateur cine film
taken the previous summer during a school trip to the
Broads where the children were given a course in life
saving. The detectives had the chance to see the real April,
not the shy girl she was with adults, but a natural, happy
child with signs of leadership and taking responsibility as
she helped the smaller children on with their lifejackets.

When the man leading the hunt saw this film he made
up his mind about what had happened to April. All week
he had considered the two possibilities, that she had run
away or been abducted. When he had seen the film, and
backed by all other information he had, he had no doubt.
She had been abducted. But by whom and how? It meant
that in a stretch of narrow country lane, no more than 300
yards at the outside, and in a matter of a few hundred
seconds, she had been snatched and taken and no one had
seen it happen, although there were people in the area.

Had someone stopped and asked her the way and
dragged her into the car? But surely someone would have
noticed it. Had she been given a lift to show someone the
way? But she would not have thrown her cycle into the
middle of a field. She did not have the strength. And
surely someone must have seen the cycle-throwing
incident. No one has ever come forward to give any
information on those matters.

The hunt went on and on. In the village church prayers
were said for her every Sunday. They were not answered.

Five months later the famous Dutch clairvoyant Gerard
Croiset came into the inquiry at the request of BBC TV.
They brought him over from Amsterdam after he had
drawn a sketch of the small Norfolk town which, he said,

April's abductor visited. He also gave a description of the man who had taken her: around 48 with a dog and carrying a gun. And his sketch gave details like a church with a main tower and two smaller ones, an ice cream parlour and a gunshop round the corner where the abductor sometimes called.

Croiset had seen all this in his home in Utrecht. He thought the dog was a 3-year-old Alsatian. The man had a grey-green Morris 1000 car. In the tree-lined square in the sun he sketched what he saw in his mind. He was an acknowledged international expert whose visions and advice had helped police solve many crimes. From his sketches police provisionally identified the town as Aylsham, a small market town just under 10 miles from where April had vanished and her bike had been thrown into the field. Mr Croiset thought the man who had done that wore mittens and had stubby fingers.

When he arrived and was taken to Aylsham he said without hesitation: 'This is the place' and he pointed out the gunshop. Sadly none of what he had seen helped the police. They followed up every scrap of information that he had given them but none of them bore any fruit. The people in the gunshop had never seen a man to match his 48-year-old with an Alsatian – or even without one.

But there has always been a problem with Mr Croiset of knowing whether what he sees is the past, present or future. This came home to the police shortly after his two day visit to Metton and the surrounding area in September 1969.

Early on 11 March 1970 the body of Susan Long, an 18-year-old insurance clerk, was found 1½ miles from her home. She had been strangled. She had been out with her boyfriend in Norwich where she worked and had caught the last bus home. When she left the bus she started to walk home but never arrived (see chapter 5). Instead she was murdered. The town? Aylsham.

And April? What of her? From the moment she disappeared until now there has been nothing. In 1990 she would be a woman of thirty-five. If she had stayed in her home area or moved away she would almost certainly be married with a family. Her children would be approaching their early teens.

No one knows whether she is alive or dead. If she was abducted, did her abductor kill her or did she lose her memory through shock and go to a city where she was lost in the crowd? Despite all means of modern communication, vast beehives of control where people are documented, their records held by numerous agencies, men, women and children by the hundred manage to lose themselves. During one hunt in Norfolk for a woman, police discovered over one hundred women who had left home and did not want to be discovered. Children do go away and sometimes come back.

Because what happened is so far fetched, it is reasonable to speculate that perhaps April was the girl on the train and the bus to London the next day. Two men who are used to observing people believe that it was her on the train. What if she had fallen off her bike, banged her head and then walked on into Cromer. She had time to catch the train. She might have lost her memory through the fall. It has happened before and will happen again. People do lose their memory and it never comes back.

Or, and very unlikely, perhaps she did have a boy friend. Girls do have secret boy friends. It might have been an older man. Perhaps she met him, perhaps something happened that so upset her that she could not go home, that she lost her memory. She might have gone to London and then met someone and she might be with them now, not knowing who she was.

Or, if one faces all the facts, she might have been taken, or gone for a ride with someone she knew, and been killed, and now lies buried somewhere in that vast expanse of Norfolk where it is so easy to hide or bury a body.

What do her parents think? How have they coped without ever knowing? When she first went they could not believe it and they were numb with the shock. They were convinced that she had been abducted. Nearly a year later, when Susan Long was murdered, Olive Fabb gave Susan's mother a message of how to cope: 'Hang on,' she said, 'keep hanging on to all the same little things, never thinking more than a few minutes ahead or you could go insane.' She and her husband were on tranquillizers, she said, but they kept it to one a day and the whole village helped in any way they could to keep them going. 'For what would happen if I went in a mental home,' queried Olive with Norfolk natural logic and commonsense, 'and April comes back to us?'

But she was bitter that if God had taken April He could have done it in a straightforward way instead of leaving them without knowing. By not knowing, by not – for instance – having a body, they could not bury her and know where she was. And in a strange way Susan's death gave her new hope, that the person who had taken their daughter might find that their conscience was so stricken that they brought her home.

Three years on, Mrs Fabb said sadly: 'Whenever I see a tall fair haired girl in the distance I wonder if it could be April and for a moment hope soars in me; but when I realize it isn't her my heart returns to normal again. Ernest and I have been experiencing this sort of pain for three years now.'

In the early days, she said, as the days and then the weeks passed and the police took over 2,000 statements which took nothing any further, they wondered if they would ever find out what had happened to April. They could not believe she had gone off on her own to meet someone. She would have worn her best clothes, taken her savings. And she was very unlikely to go with a stranger or anyone else.

The worst times were Christmas and April's birthday. 'Everything is ready for her to walk in again. Her bedroom is just the same. I've kept all her clothes and her dressing table is untouched, just as she left it. And her cairn terrier Trudy is waiting for her too. The one thing that keeps us going is the feeling that April might be around somewhere and that one day she'll come walking through the door and put the clock back three years.' She did not.

But six years after that dreadful Easter they had not given up hope. Her bedroom was untouched and there were now grandchildren. Mrs Fabb never let them out of her sight. And Mrs Fabb had only the fondest memories of her daughter who would be 20 if she was alive. Mrs Fabb had no real doubts. She said: 'I often dream pleasant dreams when it's a warm sunny morning in spring that on such a morning April will come skipping in with her own husband and little daughter and shout "Mum, I'm home".' Instead the reality was the last memory Mrs Fabb, then in her mid-sixties, had to help her keep going was April helping her with the washing up before she cycled into oblivion. She said: 'Whenever I do the washing up I remember her helping me. It was a beautiful spring day when she waved goodbye.'

The dog that April loved, Trudy, the cairn, stayed behind that day and was still there, waiting for her mistress to come back.

Time went on and on, the years changed into double figures, the Fabbs grew older, but never gave up hope, A grandchild was christened and named after April. Mrs Fabb said: 'Until they find a body I still think she's alive. I often dream and see her coming round the corner to the house.' That was after seventeen years. Her father said: 'They say time heals and I suppose it does in a way. We went through hell in those first few weeks'; and really, although he would not say it, he and his wife, patient, kind, genuine people, the salt of the very earth they lived beside in rural Norfolk, were still going through it.

Her father was insistent. 'There's no question of her going off deliberately. I sometimes sit and think what happened to her. It's bad enough when they find these children murdered but in our case we don't even know that.' Each time someone was charged with abduction in another part of the country it gave them a little bit of hope. 'You never know, someone might admit that they took April away' her mother said.

No one has. If someone did take her their will to keep silent is so strong that their conscience does not trouble them enough to give an elderly lady some peace.

Mrs Fabb said then, still in the same house, the dog sadly dead but April's room the same: 'You mustn't give up hope. It keeps you going. I think I would have been in an asylum now if I had given up hope.'

Three years later it was the twentieth anniversary. It was marked by a press conference by Norfolk police, just to acknowledge the anniversary and to let people know that inquiries were still going on, leads coming in. And the Fabbs still have not given up hope.

3

Newing

Into Thin Air

Everyone has better identifying marks than the bland descriptions police are often forced to issue when someone disappears or they are looking for a person they suspect of committing a crime. So often the facts they have to work on do not allow them to give anything other than so vague a picture that it could be one of tens of thousands or even more. 'Average build, average height, ruddy complexion with thinning hair, in his forties and wearing a blue anorak and jeans and white training shoes' is of no help to anyone.

When Steven Paul Newing vanished on 2 September 1969, five days after his eleventh birthday, and while he was playing outside his council house home in Lee Warner Avenue, Fakenham, the police were able to issue a good description. It was this: 4 feet 10 inches tall with a round face, light brown hair, blue eyes, round build, fresh complexion, medium build, thin fair eyebrows, snub nose, large ears and wearing a blue roll neck sweater with a yellow and green sweater over the top, blue jeans, baseball boots and possibly green anorak and a leather Cubs belt.

There were other things about him that came out over the years that followed (because there has been no sight of Steven from that moment until now [1991] and he would now be thirty-two years old) and they added to the picture that police were able to issue of this alert, energetic and self-assured boy. The actual photograph showed him to be as normal a boy of eleven as you can expect to find, a boy who loved animals and fishing and was often in trouble and mischief, but no more than any other boy.

The most noticeable thing is that he has lots of freckles scattered all around his nose and over it and onto his cheeks. They are the kind of freckles that cannot be missed and the type that tend to stay there forever, even if they later fade in puberty and into manhood. The next thing is the hair. It curls onto his forehead and is another small part of his make-up that makes him different from many boys – the combination of freckles and curling hair that is even more pronounced when ruffled.

Then there are the reminders of childhood accidents, a small scar over his right eyebrow where he cut himself on a glass dish when a baby, and a barbed wire scar down the back of his left leg after catching himself on a fence some years before. They are minor compared with two other injuries he collected in his hectic life in the small market town of Fakenham. These injuries involved his right arm and his teeth and were such that the police – who never stopped following every possible lead for Steven – were able to circulate details to doctors, schools and health authorities and dentists in case they came across a boy with similar ones. For his right elbow keeps coming out of joint following a fall and a break when he was seven. When it is knocked it goes out of joint again, and before his disappearance had to be reset on several occasions. But worse – and conversely better in attempting to trace him – his front teeth had to be reset after he was kicked instead of the ball in a football game. An X-ray would show the resetting and the photograph shows the small gap between them.

But most distinctive of all (and a fact that the police kept to themselves for years, as they often do in order to have something that no one else can know of – a ploy which is particularly useful in murder cases) was his bottom. He had an enormous strawberry birthmark across both buttocks. And it was actually in the shape of a strawberry. The fact that he had this mark – and will still if he is alive –

provides any person seeing it with a certainty that the man they are looking at is Steven, even if they do not have the other details to go with it. The strawberry birthmark clue was circulated to every state and private school in the country, but no one had ever seen such a distinctive mark.

Steven vanished in the September following April Fabb's Easter disappearance. His home was just off the main Norwich road and he was seen outside his home at 3.00 p.m., twenty minutes before his mother Jean came home from work. There were three other children, Terry, Christine and Debra, all grown up now.

His parents had separated. His father, Keith, was a corporal in the RAF and at one time stationed at RAF West Raynham in Norfolk, and when he came out of the services he became a fitter. He moved to Basingstoke, Hants, after he and his wife split up. His mother said that Steven did not seem particularly upset and knew where his father was and they kept in touch.

A short time before he vanished Steven had had to see the local authorities about a missing scale model aircraft kit and had been told off severely. That did not appear to bother him unduly. He was sorry that he had landed in trouble and was determined that he would not do anything like that again.

During the preceding Bank Holiday weekend he had had an argument, a row almost, with some of his friends over the ownership of a white mouse. It was not the kind of row to make a resilient boy leave home. For that was one of the first theories that the police investigated. Would he be the kind of boy to leave home after a short space of time which included a court appearance and an argument with his friends? Would he go to his father? This idea was immediately checked but Mr Newing had not seen or heard from his son.

But, the police wondered, if he had left home of his own accord, why had he not told his older brother in whom he confided or his sisters with whom he was close? The fact that he had just been playing with one friend and was on his way to another boy's home, for that is what he told his first friend, tended to discount the running away theory –

if he had done it on his own decision.

But what if he had been snatched from the roadside after walking down to the main Norwich road on that pleasant afternoon? Although it was not common in those days, not like it is now with parents afraid to let their young children out of their sight, it did happen and April Fabb was imprinted on every Norfolk policeman's mind. There had also been the case of the Lowestoft, Suffolk, family, out for a visit to grandparents in east London, coming back and stopping for a drink at one of the large pubs by the A12. Father went in to get a drink for his wife and only son, a lad aged seven and the only child they could ever have, while his wife slipped to the toilet and was back within a very few minutes. In that time the boy had been taken away into the night to satisfy the sexual urge of a man who could only find relief in such a terrible manner, and after doing so killed the boy. The man was caught and sentenced to life, but what he had done and worse, the manner in which he had taken the boy, was something that policemen remembered and tucked away in their minds.

So it was only natural that the first probe came into whether he could have been abducted. Someone going north, south, west or even east could have done it. An attractive boy, looking slightly older than his years, with an appealing smile and freckles, would catch the eye and, police had to consider, the desire of some pervert who by sheer chance happened to be passing at that moment. For months they kept up inquiries along this line; but except for two possible sightings there was nothing and never has been.

The sightings were at Sutton Bridge, just over the border north into Lincolnshire, and south, over the border into Suffolk in Kessingland, near Lowestoft. In both cases the boy whom the person who called the police thought was Steven was with a bearded man. Neither the man nor the boy has ever been found and nor have either of them ever come forward to say who they were.

Another theory that the police followed was that he had run off or had been kidnapped by the gypsies, some of whom were attending a sheep fair at Hempton near Fakenham on the afternoon that he went. His family and friends all knew of his love for animals and thought he might have gone there to have a look and joined up with them either by force or choice. The police made extensive inquiries among the gypsy and travelling families in England, Scotland and Wales but no one remembered seeing the boy and no one said they had ever taken him or been asked by him if he could join them.

There was another possibility suggested by local people, that he might have fallen down some old pits or a well in the area or one of the pits or rivers locally. His mother also felt that he might have slipped and tumbled into a sandpit or on a rubbish tip, although was unable to understand why he should have been in the area. Police frogmen searched them all, time and again, even risking their lives to search a culvert under one of the roads in the town, but again drew a blank. There were even plans some years later to search a disused well behind a sawmill which had closed and the land turned over to housing. It followed a rumour that swept the town, growing in intensity and fact as it went. It started, police discovered when they checked, when a man in a pub put forward the idea that the boy could have fallen down this well if it was still uncovered at the time Steven vanished. It was a big well, about 100 feet deep and 3 – 4 feet in diameter. By the time the story had spread through the town there was a man who had seen Steven fall down the well and the well had been left uncovered ever since and the police were going down there because they were sure that that was where his body was. The truth sadly was no more than rumour. The well was below houses that had been built over it, and from all inquiries it had been filled in long before Steven had gone in 1969.

There was another lead the police had to follow and that was one which always causes greatest anguish to innocent parents, driven to despair by what has happened. His mother was in a state of shock and under sedation. She was to say later that the first night was the worst of her life, the natural feelings of a mother, but by morning she knew he was never going to come home again. She did not believe that he had run off because she knew her son and knew he would not do such a thing.

What the police had to do was to search the family home. They did it not once but twice, to make absolutely sure that Steven was not in the house, hiding somewhere, or, although they did not suspect it, that his body might be there. It is a distasteful duty they have to carry out because they have to follow every possible idea or theory, and the most obvious place to look first is the missing child's home. It has happened in criminal history that the missing person has been found in the house. In the case of adults there have been multiple findings like Christie and the bodies of the women he had murdered in Ten Rillington Place, Notting Hill, London, but it is extremely rare with children. In this case it was not suspected and all they found was Steven's beloved fishing rods and equipment and the uniform he was due to wear when he started at Fakenham secondary school a few days after he vanished.

The Newings' home was not the only house the police searched or made inquiries at. They checked houses and homes in Fakenham, a long slog of house-to-house inquiries that has to be done and sometimes, but rarely, produces results. Many people knew the boy but no one had seen him after 3.00 p.m. on that Tuesday afternoon. Many people were only too anxious to help but they were unable to do so.

Outhouses, old buildings, farms and their buildings, heathland, moorland, forests, pools and countryside were checked. Appeals were made on television and radio in Norfolk and then, as his disappearance became linked with April as they had both vanished in the same way, there one minute, gone apparently forever the next, nationally. Each time a child disappeared nationally the two names, Fabb and Newing, joined the list. When Susan Long was murdered in Aylsham and Pamela Exall vanished on the beach at Snettisham, when the body was dumped at Cockley Cley, when anything involving mysterious unidentified bodies or children not being accounted for quickly, Steven's name comes up again. It had only one beneficial effect: that it might jog someone's memory or even make Steven think about his parents if he had in fact run off and started a new life (for reasons he had not shared with someone else) and let them know that he was alive even if he did not want to say where.

Nothing happened for nearly four years. During that time the police, led by the then head of Norfolk CID Detective Chief Superintendent Reg Lester, never stopped searching. Every possible lead was followed but there was never enough to tell them where the boy was or what had happened.

Then, one afternoon in April, 1973, Steven's father, Keith, then forty-two and working nightshifts as a fitter in Hampshire, got up, made himself a cup of tea and something to eat and sat down to watch afternoon television. He switched onto ITV and the programme he saw was called *Doing things: a day at the auction*. It was a filmed report of a pony sale at Watton, Norfolk, a town just 12 miles from Fakenham, and as Mr Newing watched he suddenly saw a face in the crowd. 'There's Steven, there's Steven' he screamed, leaping from his chair and crouching in front of the set in case the camera panned back again into the crowd. It did not. He watched until the end of the programme and saw that it had been made by Anglia Television, the Norwich-based ITV station for the eastern counties.

He immediately phoned the police, explaining to them why he was so sure that it was his son. He said later: 'It was the way his hair curled round his forehead that I noticed most. It always fell a certain way. Although the boy in the crowd had longer hair than Steven when he left home I was sure it was him. His facial features and even the ears looked the same.' The police did not waste a moment. They contacted Anglia and learnt that the film had been shot the previous September. The film was at the studios and they were only too happy to rerun it. Mrs Newing was contacted at her home and a car sent for her. The excitement, the apprehension, perhaps fear that it might not be true, were almost too much to bear.

All the files were checked to see if Watton had ever been

listed as a possible destination or place that Steven had mentioned. His parents had been there, they thought, many years ago, when Steven was small, on a visit to the RAF station but they were sure that the boy would not remember it. Both parents and police thought it unlikely that any family could have Steven in that area against his will or without being noticed, certainly not at the RAF station. The welter of publicity and the never ending hunt in the area would have pinpointed any child who suddenly appeared. Any child with Steven's distinctive description would have been noticed at once.

Just how Mrs Newing managed to contain herself in the car on the 22 mile drive to the Anglia studios in the centre of the cathedral city of Norwich is difficult to imagine. She said later that she was in a state of shock, numb with disbelief that it could be her son, clutching to the hope that it could be him. When the film was run she spotted the boy in the crowd too. The resemblance was quite striking and she gasped with the anticipation of what might now happen. She said: 'It was particularly the shape of his head, his eyes, the nose, the way his hair was cut.' The boy's father reinforced his view about the hair. 'It was the way his hair curled round his forehead I noticed most. His locks always fell onto his forehead when his hair was ruffled.'

The shot of the face in the crowd of a boy who could be Steven, the boy with a massive strawberry birthmark on his behind, lasted just two miserable seconds, the length of a blink of the eye, and if Keith Newing had blinked at that moment he would have missed the face altogether. But he did not and for the first time in forty-three long and lonely months, which both parents had suffered in different places, the mother trying to convince herself that he had been killed in a road accident but not knowing what had happened, although she was certain that he was dead, there was hope. Not a lot of hope, because the boy had to be traced and identified as Steven, but it was something, some small thing, a small straw on which to hold, a piece of hope that might just be more than that.

The two second clip was enlarged and Anglia supplied

the police with a still which was copied and circulated round East Anglia and then the rest of Britain. Other stills were made from the film of others in the crowd around the little boy who was watching the sale of the ponies so closely. For, as the officer in charge of the case at that time said: 'There is a definite resemblance between Steven and the boy on television.'

The search began for the boy and the men in the crowd. Eventually, by patient questioning and legwork, the police traced the two men. They did not know the boy and had no idea who he was or where he had come from. He was just a boy who came and stood by them in the crowd and then he went away.

The Newings did not give up the hope that they had found, but time went by and no news – either good or bad – came. It was a bad time. Mrs Newing said some time later that what people did not realize was that if a child dies the family has a funeral and that is the end. There is the grief, the mourning, the unhappiness but, after a time, however long it is, life starts to go on again and although there is a void, there is a fresh start. 'With us we still have to carry it with us. I have buried him in my mind but not in my heart. Over the years you learn to cope, to learn to live with the torment of what has happened but without ever knowing.'

A few days after the film was shown, Mrs Newing went to a pony sale at Watton with Chief Inspector Raymond Cordy, who was in charge of the investigation at that time. They walked round for hours, he a big burly Norfolk policeman with hat, scarf and pipe, she a desperate mother, fair haired, clutching her shoulder bag and keeping her fingers crossed. There were a lot of people at the sale, hundreds of them from all over East Anglia and the Midlands, and the policeman and the mother spent all day looking at faces, hoping against hope that the boy was among them. They never saw him if he was there.

Time went on and there was still no trace of the face in the crowd until, months later, when the Newings had given up hope, the boy was actually traced. It was not Steven although he did look very much like him. He came from the north of the county and had been at the sale with relatives. He was thirteen, two years younger than Steven.

Life carried on, with the mystery no nearer solved than it was the day he went. Then, ten years on, stories went round Fakenham that Steven might have fallen down an old well half a mile from his home. It was now in the back garden of a house in The Drift, a new housing development. Mrs Newing went round to have a look and the police started new inquiries and at one stage considered digging it up. But they did not do so when they learnt that it was a theory that had started the rumour, and when they investigated they discovered the well had been covered up before Steven had gone missing in September 1969. It was one of the areas near to his home, including the old quarries, that had been searched with dogs time and time again without any trace of the boy. And that is how the case stands. What did happen to the boy? Is he alive or dead? When last seen he was on his way to a friend's home. He had not given any indication that he might run off, had not told his brother that he intended to, and his mother considers that he most certainly would have done so because they were so close; he had also left his beloved fishing tackle in his room and had no money. He was not the type of boy just to run off without thought. He was resourceful, independent and adventurous. He would not have made an instantaneous decision to vanish.

So was he abducted? The bearded man seen at Sutton Bridge and Kessingland, miles apart but in that sweep of eastern England where strangers are noticed, little incidents observed and people talk among themselves, has never been traced nor the boy he was with. There was a suggestion he might have had a cream or white coloured caravanette. It might have been that he was a travelling man, a man of the roads who did not take a paper, did not have a radio or television and had no idea that the search was on. But there were posters everywhere and if he had taken the boy from outside his house or if Steven had strayed up to the Norwich road, then he would know there would be an enormous hue and cry and that he would have to keep on the move until he reached his destination or home base. Whoever he was and whoever the boy was, his son, grandson, nephew or Steven, they have never been in touch with the police and that is another part of the mystery which has never come near to an explanation.

Then there was the report that he had been seen with a woman in the Fakenham area a few days after Steven went. Police made inquiries but never found the woman nor the boy and considered that the probable explanation was that someone anxious to help find him, but who knew the boy only from the photograph in the papers and on television, made the wrong identification. It happens all the time as the public, so keen and willing to help find the missing child, report sightings that could not be that child. But at the same time the police are only too pleased to be able to check out the sightings, whether the information is right or wrong. They want people to help and sometimes what seems an impossible clue turns out to be the right one.

This happened when a baby was snatched from his pram in a shopping precinct in Essex. The mother took the baby out as usual and left her in her pram outside the shop, which mothers could do without thought back in the 1960s. But on this particular day a young woman who had lost her child decided she would take someone else's. She planned it carefully and had everything ready for the abduction and theft. For that was what it was: she intended to deprive the mother of her child forever. There was a tremendous national search for the little girl, covered extensively by the press. The mother and father, who were the first suspects naturally, but quickly eliminated once it was discovered that the mother was not suffering from post-natal depression that might make her harm her baby and the father not jealous of the child, were out of their minds with worry. But for a long time there was no trace of the little girl. The search produced blank after blank; no one could even recall seeing a woman running with the baby she had snatched from the pram. The police even called the press in to see if anyone had any fresh ideas to trace the thief and child. No one had.

But in the end the baby was found and recovered – and

the thief jailed – due to information from the most unlikely source: the Registrar of Births, Deaths and Marriages in one of the main south coast seaside towns. He had had a strange letter from a young mother-to-be in the north-east asking about registering her baby's birth in his town because of sentimental and past connections with it. When the baby was born she did register it there but the registrar thought it all very odd and made a few inquiries and then told the police that he was suspicious and that the dates might in fact tie in with those of the missing baby. His suspicion, although appearing unlikely at the start, was correct and the baby was found and reunited with its parents and has grown into a lovely young woman. The woman who stole her knew all about the anguish of the parents, their longing to have their child back, the distress she was causing. The police did not surmise this. In the boot of her car were newspapers recording what was going on in the hunt for the baby she had snatched and how it had affected her parents. Once they had the baby back they had her christened. The godfathers were the policeman who had led the search and the registrar whose sharp eye and nose for the unusual had taken police to the house where the baby was.

Unfortunately, in Steven's case there was no luck like that. But he certainly could have been taken if he had wandered up to the main road and been spotted by a passing motorist who was attracted by his freckles, fresh face and tousled hair. There are many such men about, and once he had done the awful things he wanted to he could have dumped Steven's body anywhere in the great Norfolk expanse of hiding places. Anyone who doubts that these things can happen in an instant should consider the case of a little Indian boy who had been to watch the marriage of Prince Charles to Princess Diana with his father, a solicitor. He was taken as he walked the short distance home from a shop in Putney while the au pair took his sister in to buy some sweets. The 8-year-old boy confidently set off. But a motorist stopped, turning off the A3 London to Portsmouth road via Guildford and

Goodwood where the Glorious Goodwood races were on, and took him. No one saw it happen for speed was the essential ingredient once the man had seen the little boy he fancied. How the boy was seduced into the car no one knows. Where the man took him, which side road he used off the busy A3 trunk road among the race-going traffic which joined the normal heavy stream down to Portsmouth, how he managed to assault and kill the boy without anyone noticing, how he was able to bury him in Aldgate Copse at Rogate by the A272 to Midhurst and Goodwood, the route a motorist from London would take, branching off the A3 at Petersfield to go to the races, are not known. The boy was buried and was not found for seven months. His killer has never been found.

But if not abduction or kidnap, what other options are open in the case of Steven? He could have been so delighted by what he found among the gypsies at the sheep fair that he went off with them; although why he should suddenly have taken it into his head to go there is a question that really has no answer because he had never mentioned it and had probably not even known it was on that afternoon. But although the gypsies move around and tend to avoid the taxman and the school inspector they do not live beyond the law, and if one of their number suddenly had a new son, aged 11, in their family without any reason (such as looking after the boy for relatives) someone would have noticed and told the authorities. A new-found son with such a distinctive birthmark would not have gone unnoticed.

That is true also about the idea that he went to work on a farm, his looks making him appear much older than he was. He loved animals and had talked of farms, but the same fact applies: someone would have noticed. Having noticed would they be able to ignore the publicity appealing for information about the boy or would he plead with them to let him stay and tell no one because he wanted to disappear – dozens of children surprisingly do but not often so young – and remain away from his parents? But again he was a normal little boy and he liked and loved his parents, so what would have caused the change in his normal thinking to put them through such agony?

No one can say for certain and no one has yet been able to prove whether he is alive or dead. But his mother is sure that he is dead and has said so many times, putting it this way: 'I have always believed that he is dead and did not run away. Somehow I've always thought he had an accident. I've never believed he was murdered.' She believes that he fell into one of the old quarry workings near his home on his way to his friend's house. She knows police have searched that area very thoroughly indeed. She has managed to continue after going to pieces when he first went, dreading Christmas and birthdays which are the worst moments, by treating the matter as though Steven had been killed in a road accident.

She says that although the police believe he ran away, someone must have asked questions if he was with them. 'There was no reason for him to go away. He was no angel, just a mischievous boy but I loved him. I would far rather know what happened even if it meant being certain he was dead. At least it would stop the imagination running riot.' But there has been no relief for her. No news for her is bad news. And the irony of it is that, should he be alive and she passed him in the street, she would not recognize him.

4

Headless

The Pink Nightie Non-Clue

Imagine that you have just killed your wife or girl friend. Imagine that the body is lying on the bed, the woman, *petite* and in her twenties, wearing just her pink frilly nightie, and you do not know what to do. As far as you know no one has heard you. Perhaps your home is isolated so that there are no neighbours to hear. Perhaps you have acted while she was asleep, suffocating her or possibly hitting her with an axe, a single blow killing her. Everything outside is quiet, normal, and you are standing, looking down on the woman you hated so much that you had to get rid of her and the only way to remove her is by murder.

What do you do next? In this scenario, you take the body to part of the house, the shed perhaps, under cover of darkness and there carry out the gruesome job of cutting the head off. It is a head with a mouth that undoubtedly you have kissed in love many times. You probably have the lowest light possible to do this awful job. You must have a bucket to catch the blood and you need cloths, the kind that can be disposed of easily, best by fire, to clear up the mess.

The deed is done. The body is lying there, grotesque without its head. There is still more to be done. You truss it up, with string and some sticky tape, common, easy to buy string and tape, obtainable at any shop. Then you

make the corpse into a parcel, checking first that there are
no identifying pieces of jewellery on her. No, there are
none. The nightie does not matter. She bought it at Marks
and Spencer, like tens of thousands of other women who
fancied that frilly double-layer garment.

You use an old piece of sheeting, a dust sheet of a
National Cash Register machine which has been lying
around for years, and wrap the body up and tie it ready for
disposal with some more string. You stand back and study
what you have done. There are no means of identifying
her.

You still have jobs to do. You put the head in an
ordinary shopping bag from one of the many super-
markets and put it to one side. Then you clear up,
meticulously wiping away any trace of the killing, the
decapitation. Your hatred carries you through and you do
not feel the ordinary revulsion that nearly everyone else
would.

Now you have to get rid of the two parcels. You think
about it, because the killing may have been planned for a
short while but the deed is more important than disposal,
although you have given it some thought.

Where can you dump a body and possibly get away
with it? It has to be done quickly because even in the most
remote parts there are people about. Remember the drug
smuggling gang who thought they had the perfect place,
an isolated beach on the Pembrokeshire coast? They dug a
magnificent hideaway under the beach in which to keep
their drugs as they were brought ashore, installed ship to
shore radio and were all ready to make their fortunes
when the police caught them red-handed. How? The local
fishermen had spotted them and thought they were after
their lobster pots. It was that sort of luck that you worry
about.

The sea is not suitable because the body is likely to be
washed ashore. Rubbish tips, waste ground with gravel
pits and dustbins are also out: you do not want the body
found even though the chances of identifying it are
remote. But you think you know the perfect spot. It is the
first week in August and Britain is on holiday. The roads

to the coast will be full of cars. As long as you keep your cool and do not have an accident or a breakdown you can drive almost anywhere to dump it.

And you know an ideal spot – Swaffham Forest in Norfolk, by the A1065 road that sweeps through the trees for miles from Brandon just over the border into Suffolk, to Swaffham, nearly 20 miles away. Off that road are many tracks into the trees and bracken where an unwanted parcel can be dumped. There are open spaces too like Grimes Graves, the old neolithic flint mines, and the Saxon village on Sir Peter Roberts' land at Cockley Cley. Around them the bracken is thick, the gorse a willing hiding place, and the area is remote to the ordinary traveller.

You put the parcel in the boot of your car and drive there. It is a moonlit night with not many people about, but those that are, are locals and by habit they look and watch what is going on, particularly in the dead of night.

At Cockley Cley you spot a farm track and turn off the main road quickly. In your headlights you pick out a large clump of unbroken bracken, off the track and not the sort of place where anyone will be looking. Your hands are sweating, your stomach is churning and your bowels have frozen with fear in those seconds that it takes to remove the parcel from the boot and place it in the bracken, quickly making sure that it cannot be seen but not bothering to search for an even better place. You put the car into reverse down the track, turn back onto the main road and go home, the disposal successful.

It happened, perhaps not like that, but in a similar way. It was three weeks later, on 27 August 1974, when a local farmer and his son out walking at dawn discovered the parcel because foxes had disturbed it and the victim's foot was sticking out. If the foxes had left the parcel alone it might well have stayed where it was undisturbed forever.

The farmer called the police and they came in force. The body was photographed where it was and taken to King's Lynn for a post mortem to be carried out. Without the head it was impossible to tell how she died. It also begged two questions: who was she and where was her head? The problem facing the detectives led by Detective Superintendent Ivan Mead, then deputy head of Norfolk CID, was that they had no idea who she was or where she came from.

They had the pink nightie, but that was one of 112,000 of the same size that had been sold in Marks and Spencer stores all over the country. There was no means of knowing at which store it had been bought by the headless woman, who might not even have bought it herself but been given it as a present. She might, they realized, not even be British; she might have been sent it as a present abroad. It was also possible, they suddenly and clearly saw, that the murder might not have happened in Britain at all, that the killer might have brought the body in on a car ferry, prepared to take the risk that he would not be stopped by Customs. It was a grim joke that he went through the Green Channel with nothing to declare.

The body was wrapped in a National Cash Register plastic dust sheet, 8 feet long by 5 feet 6 inches wide. It had the company crest NCR screenprinted in gold. Here, thought the police, was a real lead. Find the company who had had the machine and this cover and there was a trail to follow. They found the company who manufactured the cover. It was in Dundee and it had gone into liquidation six years before. It was one of hundreds that had been manufactured to cover calculating machines made between 1962 and 1968. It was an impossible task.

Then there was the string and the sticky tape. It was the kind that could be bought anywhere in the British Isles. Whoever had dumped the body had done a very efficient job.

So the police turned to the missing women files. There were dozens of missing women in the age and height range of the headless lady (and where was her head and why had nobody reported a woman of her description being missing during August? For no one did).

Norfolk police had twelve missing women to follow up. Methodically, and with great persistence, they traced every one of them, and the women were not best pleased.

They had left home for a variety of reasons and did not want those they had left behind to trace them. Nationally the police did even better, finding over 100 women who were on the missing list, and again they were angry that they had been traced, having gone to a great deal of trouble to make sure that they were not discovered. Why did they go? Domestic trouble, a husband they did not love any more, a new man, debts that had become too much and were about to be discovered, a longing just to be on their own and to start a new life, the children too much, loss of memory, loss of will to go on in familiar surroundings ...

Nationwide publicity produced absolutely nothing to help identify the body. The police interviewed 15,000 people and 7,000 questionnaires were filled in during house-to-house inquiries, but the sum of the findings was nil. No one could help.

It is (so far) the perfect disposal of a body, but not a perfect murder, because a perfect murder is one where no one knows that it has been committed. But if the murder is such that once the body has been found, the pathologist will know what has happened, then disposal becomes necessary. And in that context this is a classic of its kind. Bodies are often dumped around the countryside. Mrs Diane Jones, wife of an Essex doctor, was left, undiscovered for months. Little Linda Smith, taken from the roadside in Essex, was left strangled at Polstead, just over the border into Suffolk, near the site of the Red Barn where William Corder murdered and buried the body of Maria Marten and achieved international immortality by doing so. They and many others were found, probably due to the desire of the killer to get rid of the corpse and get the hell out of it as fast as possible, knowing that the body will be found but leaving no clues to connect it to him or her.

In this case there was planning to make sure the body was not found and it was pure chance that it was. But the killer had made absolutely certain that it would not be identified by removing every object identifiable and by knowing that no one was going to ask any questions when the woman went missing or by being sure that he had the skill to convince those who did ask that the woman had gone away on her own voluntarily and wanted to disappear. It is not a difficult or uncommon thing to do.

Sometimes killers dispose of the body in a well thought out way, like this headless lady killer. Another such crime happened just over the border into Suffolk in the early 1960s when a farm worker discovered two suitcases behind a hedge in a field just off the A12 London to Ipswich road at a place called Tattingstone, not far from Ipswich. Inside the suitcases were eight pieces of a human body, cut up with exceptional skill, suggesting that the person who did it had surgical knowledge. When the post mortem took place and the body was put back together, the pathologist discovered he had the corpse of a 16-year-old boy.

This time the killer had left the head but no clothing at all. Perhaps he thought that leaving the head of this poor boy would not help police because they would not be able to circulate the description. Such descriptions do not help much because they are invariably so similar to other boys of that age. But the killer miscalculated. The police could do better than words. They could photograph the head, gruesome task that it was.

The national press was there in force, covering this macabre story. Among them was a very experienced photographer called Freddie Girling who had seen murder and death both as part of his job and in the war. Suffolk police talked over what they wanted to do with Freddie and one or two of the other senior photographers there and Freddie said he could see a way of taking a picture of the boy's head. He and a police photographer set up the shot, using glycerine to make the eyes look alive, and when they had taken the picture it was passable. It looked like the head, but attached to the body, of a teenage boy, and if you looked carefully you could see he was dead. If you glanced and did not recognize him, you would not know that it was the head that was part of an eight piece package so horrifically left behind a hedge.

It had immediate results. On his way home the boy's

father saw the picture on the front page of the now defunct *Evening News*, one of the London evening papers. It must have been the most awful moment in his life to see his dead son's photograph staring out from the front page of the paper. He went to the police and later that evening had the heart breaking task of confirming that the picture he had seen was that of his son whose body was lying on the Ipswich mortuary slab in front of him.

But the killer still got away with the crime. He was never caught. The boy, who came from north London, had vanished from home a fortnight before his body was found and police think that he might have been enticed by a gang of homosexuals who were (and still are) operating in central London, chatting up boys who hang around amusement arcades and luring them with talk of parties, drink, cigarettes and possibly drugs to parties where, once under the influence of drink, they are encouraged to take part in homosexual practices. The boy may well have objected or said that he would go to the police, and that signed his death warrant. Whatever happened, he died and was dumped like old rubbish in the countryside miles from home.

Police never did find out what happened to him after he left home. A homosexual who preyed on youths died later and they suspected it was him. He had medical skills but there was never any proof.

5

Long

The Man at the Bus Station

When the No. 10 bus pulled out of Norwich bus station at
10.25 p.m. on 10 March 1970, it was the last time Susan
Long, a pretty dark-haired 18-year-old, planned to be
aboard. Her season ticket to Aylsham, 12 miles and 50
minutes away, expired that night and the next morning
she was going to drive her 6-year-old Vauxhall Viva to her
work at Norwich Union, the vast international insurance
company where she worked in the addressograph
department. For months she had saved for the car which
would give her independence from public transport.

She had enjoyed a lovely evening with her boy friend,
Brian, who was also eighteen. They both worked for
Norwich's biggest employers, and for both of them it was
their first romance. It was idyllic, it was fun and they
rejoiced in each other's happiness. They talked of getting
engaged in about a year's time.

Four times a week they spent time together after work.
Susan stayed on in Norwich before catching the last bus.
That Tuesday night they went to the Gala Ballroom in
Norwich, a happy young couple in love, laughing and
dancing the night away. Brian walked her to the bus and
kissed her goodnight before she boarded the bus with
about a dozen other passengers. Just before it left a man
ran to the single decker and tapped on the window to try
to attract someone's attention. Then he hurried away,

perhaps to a car that was parked nearby. The police have never been able to find out who the man was, who the owner of the car was, where the car went. For if they had been able to they might be able to solve another of Norfolk's great mysteries.

The bus made its way to the small market town of Aylsham. When it pulled into the market place Susan got out and began the seven minute walk to her home in Sir William's Lane. She was an only child, an only grandchild too, and lived there happily with her parents, Derek, a carpenter, and her mother Molly, a canteen worker. Susan was a tall girl, 5 feet 10 inches, and good looking, a smart dresser. She wrapped her black mini-coat with silver buttons round her as she left the bus at 11.14 p.m. She should have been home by 11.20 p.m. but she never arrived. Instead, she was found around 5.30 a.m. by a milkman who only just saw the body, lying face down in a puddle, in time and was able to pull up. He knew that she was dead.

Once again, Detective Chief Superintendent Reg Lester, then head of the CID, was called in to lead the hunt for the killer. A post mortem established that she had been strangled. She had not been sexually assaulted but it was obvious that sex was the motive because no one is going to pick up an attractive girl in a sleepy Norfolk market town at 11.15 p.m. just for the company.

The spot where Susan ended her short life was a local lovers' lane. When police examined the area, just 1½ miles from her home, they found her blue and white bracelet was missing and one of her size six blue sling-back shoes.

From the start of the inquiry the police were reasonably certain that the crime was committed by a local person. There were several reasons for this, the main one being that Susan would not have accepted a lift from a stranger under any circumstances and certainly not late at night. This may have been 1970 in a law-abiding town where violence was unheard of but girls still knew the risks of accepting lifts. And what would be the point? She was only a few hundred yards from her home. So she would only take a lift from someone she knew. Another reason was that the spot where she was dumped was known to locals but not to someone casually visiting the area. It was reasonable to think that the person who gave her a lift and killed her knew her and it was because of that that she got into the car and suddenly found that the man she thought was a friend wanted sex. He drove past the area where she lived and another 1½ miles further on. Did Susan fight? Did she tell him that she would tell his wife or family and that the only way he could silence her was to kill her?

Around 4000 people lived in Aylsham or the surrounding area and Chief Superintendent Lester and his men knew that it was going to be a long, hard and persevering case of elimination. There were some clues and leads. There were the fourteen other people who travelled on the bus that night. What had they seen? There was the man who ran forward and tapped on the window and then went to the car that stood on its own. The only description of it was that it was a Mini. Could that have been the car of a boy friend whom Susan had met but had kept secret, a boy who then got into his car and raced ahead of the bus to meet up with her at journey's end. There was a report that a car had hooted its horn when the bus arrived, but that was a Ford.

But all inquiries showed that no one knew anything of another man in Susan's life, that she had eyes only for Brian and he for her and it was almost impossible that she would have a date with another boy the night she had danced with the boy she loved and planned to marry. She was just not that kind of girl. She was straight, honest and a former Sunday school teacher. The idea of leading a secret love life would just not enter her head.

Police made the usual appeals, helped by enormous local and national publicity because Aylsham was so close to where April Fabb had vanished less than a year before, and asked for any information, anyone who had suspicions about loved ones, neighbours, anyone who could help in any way to come forward. They particularly wanted the driver of the car parked at the Norwich bus depot, the man who hooted his horn at Aylsham, the man who tapped on the window of the bus at Norwich and the man who they learnt had been parked in a lane by the sewage farm not far from the lane at Brough, around 12.30 a.m. to come forward. None of them ever has.

They were also interested in the Ford which they think had been resprayed or repainted in metallic maroon, but it was never traced.

There was only one thing to do and that was to ask every person in the town – and there were 3,670 of an age able to answer questions – what they knew, if anything, and could they help in any way. Put like this it sounds a hard but not too difficult task. In fact that kind of house-to-house inquiry which involves visiting every house is time consuming and a slog, part of a detective's work that is not shown on television. There the viewer sees a policeman call at a selected house where the householder is always in and always answers the questions and always supplies the information that is required. If they do not supply the information, another officer is round soon afterwards and the information is supplied then.

In reality the task is arduous. Take a street of thirty houses with four people living in each, all of whom have to be questioned. Perhaps the detective who calls during the day is lucky and finds twenty of the women of the house in. But in the other cases they will be at work like their husbands and children, or the children will be at school. So the detective goes back with his pro forma, which lists all the questions which have been drawn up by his superiors, at evening meal time with the hope that all the occupants he has not already seen will be in. Most are but one husband is working late, it's soccer practice for some sons, choir practice for daughters, youth club night, mother's night out at the bingo and she's gone early. So the detective makes do with the people in the house and asks his questions and makes an appointment to see the others the next day, and goes back again and most are there but there may be one or two who have not been able to make it home in time so he has to wait or come back later in the evening ...

What he wants to know is: where were you after 10.30

p.m. on Tuesday 10 March? If you were at home, who can tell us that you were? If you were out, where were you and with whom; can you name them and give their address? If you were on your own, where did you go and did you see anyone who can vouch for the fact that you were there, and why were you there? And why were you out at such a time on your own if there is no one who can say you were there? Have you heard anything about anyone who was out and about after 10.30 p.m. that night and why they were out? And did you know Susan Long and do you know any of her friends?

Once the detective has asked the questions 120 times for just one street in the town all the information that he has obtained, negative or positive, has to be collated at the Incident Headquarters and matched with all other information that has come in the same way. Thus if Mr A says that he stayed talking outside the pub with his friends Mr B and Mr C until 11.15 p.m. and on walking home with Mr C they crossed the market place at 11.17 p.m. and saw a dark car parked near the bus stop, that would have to be checked with B and C and they might say they saw D and E, and E may say that on his way home he saw Mrs A with a Mr H, and all those people have to be seen to check that what the others have said is right. And so a picture is built up in the way a map may be made, showing just who was where and when on the night of the murder in the sleepy town in the depths of a sleepy county.

All this was done and it took hours and hours and involved dozens of detectives. While they did it in Aylsham another team went round everyone who could possibly have known the dead girl in Norwich at her workplace and at the dance hall, those who had been on the bus, those who came forward to say they had seen her on her way to the bus. There were no computers to help in those days.

By now Scotland Yard had come into the investigation in the form of Detective Chief Superintendent John Cass. It was the practice of some chief constables in those days to call in one of Scotland Yard's Murder Squad to take over a murder inquiry which was causing difficulties. It used to cause resentment in some cases. On one occasion the head of another county CID kept the Man from the Yard waiting while he finished taking a confession from the killer before flourishing the statement in an outstretched hand of welcome to tell the London man that he had wasted his journey because the locals had beaten him to it.

The Man from the Yard on this case had no such problems and there was fine co-operation with the Norfolk force. But he might well have wished to have had a signed confession handed to him when he arrived because he never had another chance.

The house-to-house inquiries produced 10,000 statements and nothing else. There was a mass of information but none took anyone any closer to Susan's killer.

The police tried another line of inquiry. They knew that Susan had fought for her life, a fact they did not immediately divulge, and that they had a sample, a trace, of the murderer's blood. Six weeks after the murder they decided to take a blood sample of every man and youth in the town. No one objected and if the killer was among them he was not going to draw attention to himself in any way, because the town had become a place of suspicion with rumour rife and everyone asking themselves 'Is it him? Could it be him?'; because all were certain that it must be a local man unless Susan did have a secret friend and that was so ridiculous as to be totally discounted.

For days during May a team of four doctors took a sample of blood from all the males at a small centre set up in the market place. Most came without any reminder. A few took a little longer, not because they were guilty but because they did not like the idea. At the end of a week all the men had given a sample and they were sent off for analysis at the forensic laboratory at Nottingham. It did not help. There was no definite link so that police could go to a man and say 'Could we talk to you again, please.'

There was no sign of her shoe, no trace of her bracelet. Time moved on and other things occupied the minds of the people of Aylsham, except for Susan's grieving parents and boy friend, the police and the man who had killed her and had managed to cover his guilt by keeping silent, with his own conscience the only means of making him confess.

From time to time there would be another murder of a teenage girl and police would check to see if there could be a link. There was one case in Cheshire where there could have been a link because police thought the killer might be travelling the roads and motorways of England, picking up his victims as he went. But Susan's murder was considered too far from the main network to be really involved.

In July 1971, sixteen months after the murder and a major investigation which had yielded nothing concrete to the detectives who had worked so hard, a possible lead turned up in a lodging house in Norwich. It was a screwed-up note, barely legible, scrawled in ballpoint, inside a bookmaker's envelope in which had been placed £114 in winnings. The note was clearly written by someone under great stress and referred to girls and what he might or might not do to them. It did not mention Susan by name but it was enough for police to try to trace the man.

Their inquiry led them nowhere but it brought up another lead. The story of the note appeared in one of the Sunday newspapers and it was seen by a woman with a nagging secret. She wrote an anonymous letter from Cambridge, saying that she had been in the area of lovers' lane at Brough with a man who was not her husband around 11.30 p.m. on the night Susan was driven off to her death. She had seen a speeding car, driven by a man who looked very frightened and strange, and she followed him. Although she was in a Cortina, she had great difficulty in keeping up with him and finally lost him. She gave a vague description of the car she followed which was in such a terrible hurry.

The reason why she had not told anyone before, she explained in the letter, was because she was still with her husband at the time and he did not know what she had been up to that night. Now she was separated and seeing the new story about the gambler's scribbled ramblings had made her decide to break her silence. It was the only time that she did, for, although police appealed to her, they did not hear from her again.

This was a pity because it could have been of great help. If it was 11.30 p.m. when she saw the car racing along and followed it, it could possibly fit the times, provided that the killer picked up Susan around 11.12 p.m., drove her to the lovers' lane and that, when she saw what he was about and began to fight and he began to strangle her, only a very short time had passed. It could well have all been done in less than twenty minutes – the pick up, the drive, the killing, the casual dumping of the girl in the mud and water and then racing away to the sanctuary of his home. He knew the roads, the local short cuts and double-back routes, and if someone was following him he could lose them.

The fact that it had taken seventeen months, a broken marriage, a newspaper story in a paper which in those days followed unsolved murders with regular stories, to jog a woman's memory is one of the problems that detectives face in their inquiries. A woman with a man who is not her husband, the man with another man's wife, going to a quiet spot to have illicit sex, even in this liberal age where marriage to many is of very little worth, are still not keen to come forward and tell what they saw, preferring their secret to remain with them and not take the chance that it might, despite police promises that their identity will be kept secret, come out and lead to complications that they do not want or deserve – like murder by a jealous partner.

Modern means of communication have made such situations possible. Computer information cannot be guaranteed secret and the wrong person may get to know. It is a risk that secret lovers are not always prepared to take, thus hindering an inquiry by not revealing information that might possibly be vital at the time.

It is not only fear of others knowing that holds people back. Many dislike the police enough not to help them. A few years ago near Southampton, a son walked round a housing estate with a shot gun under his arm to go and kill a divorced man who was his mother's lover. Several people saw him, others heard the shot and came out of their houses, leaving their suppers cooking on the stove, and saw the youth break the gun and walk away with it, leaving the man dying in his hallway. The killer was followed by a group of boys, eager to see what would happen next. It was just like television. But hardly anyone bothered to tell the police. The reason was one of hatred for the police, although it was not a particularly criminal estate, not because they did not want the killer caught. As far as they were concerned it was none of their business.

In Susan's case, many people did think it was their business and they hurried to help but to no avail. But there were others who might be in the position of the woman who wrote from Cambridge because of the information she had kept nagging away at her until she had to tell.

There was, and is, certainly one person who kept his silence. People may well ask how it is possible for him to live with it, how he can keep it secret from his wife or those he lives with, parents perhaps. They think that way because they know that *they* could not live with it; but a murderer can and there is no reason why his wife should know. There are many wives who have no idea what their husbands do.

6

Reddin

Do Anything But Don't Hit Me Again

Some roads stick in your memory for a variety of reasons. Some because they are fast and a bore, a route on which to get on with the journey and finish it as quickly as possible. Many motorways are like that, grinding tension-filled ways of going from A to B with you, the driver, hoping there will not be a crash and that if there is one you will not be involved, and that the jam will not last too long. Other roads are full of beautiful scenery so that, although not travelling fast, the time slips away in the pleasure of what you can see. Others remain fixed in your mind because of stops on the way. The A10 for me was such a road.

When I covered East Anglia for a national newspaper in the days before car phones, it was a firm rule that you had to ring in every hour when you were travelling. As I often travelled the A10 from Cambridge to King's Lynn, I knew it – the phone boxes and the watering holes (in the days before the breathalyser when you could stop at a pub for a quick one as you phoned without the worry of the police sniffing your breath) – very well indeed. One pub in Downham Market was a favourite, particularly on market day. In those days if you knew your way round East Anglia you could drink every day all day, except Sunday. You could do it in Norfolk but they had a tendency there to close for a while late afternoon to let the locals get their breath back. In parts of Suffolk they were like the Windmill and never closed.

However, this pub had a roaring open fire and a phone box in the hall and a large car park just off the main road because the A10 went through the town centre and the market place. It was in the bar of this pub that one afternoon two men came in while three of us were all making a check call to our newspapers on our way home from a court case in King's Lynn. One asked for champagne, any champagne, and the owner of the pub looked bemused because he was not often asked for champagne – good ale, the occasional malt whisky, but not champagne. The other man was bemused and overloaded. In his pockets were fivers and tenners by the hundred and they were spilling out onto the floor. His friend picked one up and offered us a drink. He mentioned that they were not a pair of robbers but his friend was the owner of the 2000 Guineas winner and they were on their way back from Newmarket where they had cleaned up. We drank with them until the landlord appeared with some very dusty bottles from his cellar and that of a nearby hotel.

Further down the road, if the traffic was with you and the tractors and the sugar beet off the road, you could make it to Hilgay or, if you were really lucky, to Brandon Creek to a box just below the high bank of the River Ouse, a mighty protection built up after the nightmare floods of 1953 which made the whole area a sea and killed people and animals and wrecked homes and land. From there on it was on to Littleport and then the cathedral city of Ely where the road improved and the last stretch to Cambridge or towards Newmarket was fast and easy. I mention all this for a particular reason. As I drove along it for years there were always girls hitch hiking. I do not know why I should remember that because I never gave lifts, but when a 14-year-old from Downham Market was reported missing fifteen days after going off to Hilgay to see her boy friend with her taxi fare in her hand and the taxi booked to pick her up by the war memorial later in the evening, I knew immediately what had happened. She had been hitching a lift and she had gone and was following in the pattern of that area of Norfolk, vanishing like April Fabb and Steven Newing and Pamela Exall (see Chapter 7). One minute she was by the roadside, just on the edge of the town, and then she was gone.

It was 15 December 1976. Heidi, an attractive, busy teenager who loved dancing and going to pubs to listen to the music over soft drinks, had had a row with her boy friend Kevin, aged eighteen, who lived in Hilgay, 3 miles out of town, the evening before. On 15 December she decided to go over there and patch up the quarrel. She borrowed a pound from her grandmother and went into town to book a taxi to bring her home at 9.30 p.m. Then she went to see some friends in one of the market place hotels before setting out just after 7.30 p.m. to thumb a lift to Hilgay.

Police waited fifteen days before starting a major press campaign to find her. During that time, which stretched over Christmas, her parents were frantic with worry. The police made every inquiry they could to see if she could have gone off with someone voluntarily, could have gone to relatives, could be in hiding. All the time the thought of what had happened to April and Steven hung over them. They knew that as soon as it was made public, the disappearance would be linked to those two, comparisons would be drawn, the past cases would be brought up again. It was a terrible Christmas.

Finally, on 30 January, Norfolk police held a press conference to announce that another young girl in that waste land of Norfolk had gone, vanished in a puff of wind. In a county where there are 2 acres for every member of the population – and in reality much more because over a third live in Norwich – it was a frightening fact. This, in a small area, was the fifth case in seven years: four gone totally, the fifth found murdered but no killer caught.

Detective Chief Inspector Charles Nourse, a Norfolk man who knew the area well and all about the other cases, said: 'We are very concerned about her, particularly with a history of these other people. She has disappeared like the others.'

Until it became a national crime, the inquiry had followed the normal pattern in such matters. The first person to be seen was the boy friend. He was a pleasant teenager and he could tell the police that not only did Heidi not call at his home, but that he had no idea that she was coming and had spent all evening at home. The taxi firm confirmed that they had sent a car to Hilgay for the pick-up time but the girl did not appear, and after waiting for a while the driver returned to the office. Her friends were seen. She had met them in the hotel and then had left about 7.30 p.m., they said. Later a witness told the police that they had seen the girl hitch hiking on the A10 around that time.

The mystery was compounded – and gave hope – because on the afternoon of the day after she had failed to return home, two people were sure they saw her in Downham Market. One was the friend of her father, the other an old school friend. They did not speak to the girl whom they thought was Heidi – 5 foot 5 inches tall, blonde, striking to look at – but were initially sure it was her. Later it turned out they were mistaken.

The papers and television naturally linked all the disappearances together. Was a maniac at large? Some added in the headless body at Cockley Cley, but that had no bearing. Every avenue the police had followed on that showed it was not committed by someone in Norfolk but from outside. Missing women in Norfolk tend to be noticed.

That left April and Steven and Pamela and Susan, four names that everyone in Norfolk knew. Police reasoned that Steven was not really part of the link because if someone was going round abducting girls, it was for one reason only. He would not be interested in a little boy. Heidi had one feature in common with April and that was that they were striking looking girls in an attractive way and about the same age, ready to bloom. Susan was older but had in common with April the fact that she would not take a lift from a stranger. Heidi was not like that. She would hitch hike and join the other girls who did so on the A10 as often the only way to get around for those without a car in the evenings because of the poor bus service.

Pamela did not fit into any of these categories, and her story is told in the next chapter. She may either have been abducted by someone who chanced upon her by accident – and that was a theory police had to consider because that was what had happened in the cases of April, Susan and Heidi – or she may have been caught by the tide and drowned. That seemed the most likely explanation.

So the police were left with two distinct possibilities: one person was responsible for all three, or they had three men all behaving the same way, roaming the area or, if not roaming, very well acquainted with it, and dangerous.

The days turned into weeks. Heidi's parents were frantic with worry about their only child. The police followed every clue but, as with April and Susan, they led nowhere. The break-through came on Saturday 30 January when two boys were out hunting for old bottles so they could go and collect the deposit on them. They were peering into the ditch near Sandpit Hill, an old strip of tarmac used by lovers beside the back Denver – West Dereham road which is just off the A10, a spot well known to locals but not to outsiders (as in Susan Long's murder in Aylsham) and 2 miles from Heidi's home. As they poked around for precious bottles they disturbed some under-growth and found a body. They called the police and the search for the missing girl was over. She was lying face down in the water, her body only partly clothed with some odd marks on her bare bottom. They suggested some gruesome mutilation.

When the pathologist arrived it was obvious to him that the body had been there some time. It was almost certain that it was dumped there on the night she disappeared, six weeks before.

In the ditch with her were all her clothes, also carefully concealed, all but her left-hand leather glove. The killer had taken that with him or it was in his car. The pathologist found another interesting clue: there were dog hairs on the girl's body.

Three months before Heidi was so cruelly murdered dustman Peter Hunter appeared before the magistrates at Downham Market and pleaded guilty to indecently assaulting a 26-year-old housewife called Belinda in a car park at night. He was chased off by her husband and at first charged with attempted rape, but this was withdrawn. He pleaded guilty to indecent assault and assault occasioning actual bodily harm. The case lasted half an hour and Hunter, moustached and handsome, left the court with his wife Pamela to go back to his council house home and black labrador dog in Paradise Road.

What had happened? Later his victim was to tell how the man from Paradise Road grabbed her hair and warned: 'Don't scream, don't shout, don't do anything and I won't kill you.' He kicked her in the face and lashed her across the back with a heavy dog lead, with his dog beside him, she said, as he pulled her down and knelt on her. Then her husband came along and Hunter ran off but was caught. He was fined £120 with £10 compensation.

Some months later it was revealed that while awaiting trial he had gone round the small town, telling people he was innocent, even kneeling before his victim's mother to tell her that 'as God is my judge' he had not assaulted her daughter. In court he pleaded guilty and months afterwards the chairman of the magistrates said they would not have acted any differently in fining him because he was a man in his twenties, happily married with a stable background. They would have had to put him in prison to stop what happened next, and there is no doubt that a prison sentence was not called for. An alternative to a fine like probation would not have deprived the man from Paradise Road of his freedom. So he was a free man with no restrictions when he saw Heidi hitch hiking on the A10 and stopped to give her a lift.

When the police went round to see him – as they did with many people in Downham Market, but a man with a previous conviction for assault on a woman was an obvious person to talk to – he admitted that he had killed her. When the case came to trial at Norwich crown court and Hunter pleaded not guilty to murder and rape, the jury heard two facts that had not been revealed to the public before: that Heidi was alive when he threw her into the ditch after trying to strangle her, and she died from drowning, and that after death he mutilated the body by carving a noughts and crosses pattern on her bare backside. The cuts in her left buttock were cut by a left-handed man. Hunter was right-handed but had told the police that he used his left hand to cut food.

It was all very civilized in the crown court. It was ten months on and everyone was smartly dressed, well behaved and soft voiced. There was none of the terror the screams and violence that preceded the killing of a 14-year-old girl who was so frightened that she pleaded with the man who had picked her up, that she said he could do anything as long as he did not hit her again. It cost her her life.

The trouble with a court is that it is so different to the event about which those present are hearing. Everything is so clean, so orderly, even so old fashioned. Presiding is a middle aged or elderly man in a wig and red robes, something that might be considered as fancy dress by anyone irreverent enough to say so. He has the power, almost, of God Almighty. Below him sits another man in a wig but this time in a black robe who is the clerk of the court. He too has massive powers but not nearly as much as the judge. Sitting in rows and facing the clerk are the barristers, who have no powers except the right to address the judge and jury, and they too wear wigs and black gowns. In front of them they have bundles of photocopied documents, statements of evidence, plans, maps, occasionally bundles still wrapped in pink ribbon. They often have exhibits, deadly knives in cellophane packets, guns, whips, hairs, pieces of clothing that were once worn with comfort but are now soiled and stained, books of photographs that are sometimes in black and white but increasingly in colour. They show various things like – in this case – the car, the scene of the crime, the ditch and, most important, the girl, the dead girl as she was in the ditch, as she was as she was pulled out, as she was on the mortuary slab, photographs to sicken the most hardened detective. But they are in the sort of albums you might have at home and can quickly be shut. A squeamish jury member, and they are all squeamish when it comes to looking at something so revolting and heart-breaking, can freeze the eyes so they do not take in the full horror. A dead body, particularly of a pretty girl, does not look very real on the page of an album in a centrally heated court room where everyone is discussing the details in a rather matter of fact way to anaesthetize the bestial thing that has been done, and can be seen without the smell and the reality of the pathetic dead victim.

Behind the barristers are the instructing solicitors, smartly dressed men and women in black suits, with bundles of photocopied documents alongside them. They know all the details because they have taken statements from the client and been there when the barrister has spoken to the client. The prosecution instructing solicitors know as much too because they have prepared the brief for the barrister on all the available evidence.

Behind them in the dock sits the defendant, the client of the defending barrister. He is the one who is left alive out of the meeting that put a 14-year-old girl in the ditch. It could have been another person charged with murder for this is another day in the life of the court which sits, with breaks for holidays which grow shorter every year as the crime rate soars, round the clock, year in year out. But this defendant, as many other defendants, looks quite different to his appearance on the night he is said to have raped and killed a schoolgirl.

Defendants who are burglars, rapists, armed robbers, vandals, yobbos, football hooligans or just people who like sticking knives and boots into the bodies of fellow citizens, do not appear in court in their working gear. They do not come casually dressed. They are as dressed up for the occasion as everyone else in court. When out committing their crimes they will have worn casual clothes, such as jeans, with perhaps heavy boots and concealed knife (the yobbo), balaclava and anorak (the armed robber), club t-shirt and scarf (the football hooligan), or unidentifiable, disposable clothes (the rapist). But when they come into the dock at the crown court there is a uniformity of dress as though they were going to work at a bank or office where a suit, shirt and tie and clean shoes are the regulation outfit. In the dock they appear clean, smart, hair cut, clean-shaven (apart from a moustache), fitting into the tableau.

They do not shout when they give evidence or from where they sit, flanked by two prison officers. Only the most outrageous break the rules and yell at the judge or witnesses, and this is usually because the evidence, in their view, is so terribly wrong or they think the judge is biased.

And so it was on 26 October, 1977 that Hunter of Paradise Road, Downham Market, made up the set piece for the day and the few that followed it, smartly dressed, smartly suited among the wigs and gowns and other suits. What the jury, who also came smartly dressed because they too are part of this ritual of old England that has been slightly modernized in action but not in dress over the years, heard was frightful; though if you looked around it was difficult to imagine it in these surroundings. Oh yes, it was all set out factually, nicely, oh so nicely. The sheer evil of what Hunter, dog lover, happily married man, had done was detailed. But, did the jury wonder, did this nice looking young man really do this on a December night in Norfolk? A half naked girl, strangled, raped, mutilated, left in a ditch, hidden in a ditch to make sure that she was not found, but by mischance she was. In the snug warmth of the court in a beautiful city it was a far cry from the lonely lane on a cold night where a big man was murdering a young girl.

I said before that the trouble with a court was the fact that it is the opposite of what they are hearing. What happened was full of passion, hatred, fear, lust, evil; but these events are explained and related in a cold careful unemotional way in a court, staged in almost theatrical imagery. The way the facts are presented and argued over, denied or admitted, is done in a way that has been followed for years and works. The excitement and shouting, bullying and dramatic scenes, well known from American television plays and series, do not occur here. It is as low key as the stiff upper lip and it is rare that the defendant lets the side down when he is sentenced. So it was when the prosecutor, Mr Michael Beresford West, QC, stood to open the case for the crown and tell the jury what the prosecution said had happened and what they intended to prove.

The circumstances were as I have already related. Because she had had a tiff with her boy friend Heidi decided to hitch hike to Hilgay to see him and patch up their quarrel. Hunter was one of many people seen after she vanished and later was seen by police again. And this time he admitted it was he who had killed her. He said in a statement to the police that he panicked and hit her soon after picking her up as she hitched on the A10 because he thought she had recognized him. Then, he was alleged to have told the police: 'She said you can do what you want but don't hit me again. I'll tell everyone I fell over.'

He was asked if he had taken her to West Dereham, where she was found, and he said: 'Yes, yes, Christ I am sorry.' Then he was asked whether he put her into the dyke and he said: 'Oh hell, yes I did.' Then he told the police why. He took her to a favourite courting couples' spot, where a car similar to his was seen by a passing woman (she thought it was a dark Maxi and that was the kind of car Hunter had, said the prosecutor) and there they had sex. And afterwards, he said: 'I got the belt of her coat, put it round her neck and pulled, I just panicked and smacked her one then put her in the dyke.' Just like that. He had his way, she was under age, he panicked, he smacked her one, this girl barely into her teens and frightened with very good reason out of her wits, and threw her into the dyke, half dressed, throttled but still alive, to drown in the mucky waters, rodent infested and full of pesticide.

The man in the white wig and the black robe called his witnesses to prove what he had told the jury so that when they had heard all the evidence they could make up their minds beyond all reasonable doubt that the man from Paradise Road, who now sat smartly dressed in his suit in the dock, had done this thing. The bundles of photographs were handed round and inspected. A forensic scientist had evidence to show that fibre on the girl's clothing matched the carpet and seat cover in Hunter's car; also on her clothing were dog hairs, hairs from a big black dog, Hunter's black dog.

The police told how Hunter made the statement to them admitting rape and murder but denying that he had mutilated the girl's bottom after death. No, he had not done that.

Then Hunter gave evidence and he denied that he had murdered Heidi and said that he had only told the police that he had done so 'because I could not see how anybody would believe me that all I had done was to pick her up'. Now he had a different story as was his right, under oath, in the witness box. He had told the police originally he was sorry that he had dragged her out and thrown her into the ditch and that she was dead then: 'after what I had done with the belt to her, she was not moving any more'. But when told that in fact she was alive and had drowned he broke down and cried and said 'Oh Christ, no.'

Now he told the jury that he had given her a lift but during the journey she had made a comment that upset him when asking to be let out of the car. 'I took it the wrong way. I'm afraid I lost my temper and I hit the girl' he said. 'I gave her my handkerchief to clean herself up. She was bleeding either from her nose or her mouth. I can't say which.' She then got out of the car and he saw her walking towards Hilgay before he drove off, never to see her again.

The jury did not believe him and he was found guilty and jailed for life for the murder and for eight years for the rape; the rape sentence was to run concurrently with the life sentence. Mr Justice Croom-Johnson told him: 'There are varying degrees of rape and this was a perfectly dreadful one.' Then the defendant in his best suit was taken to the cells, the gentlemen in the dress of another age left the court, and the others involved who had come to judge only that trial left the court too and went home, hoping never to have to return. Those who are part of the legal system were back again the next morning for another trial.

And Hunter? Why did he do it? What made a happily married man – for his wife, Pamela, aged twenty-three, and he were happy and after the verdict she said she did not believe it and she was sticking by him – do such a dreadful thing? Was it the sight of a girl whom he had seen before and been attracted to, that made him stop when he picked her up in his headlight beam? What was he doing out anyway and what made him rape her and, even worse, throw her into the ditch and then, when she was dead, drowned not strangled as he had intended, cut those marks on her backside?

Poor little girl, a victim of an attack that she could not imagine happening. Some girls carry weapons to ward off such an attack if it should occur while they take such a terrible risk. There is nothing new in girls hitch hiking and being found later dead by the roadside or attacked and raped and left a shivering, naked wreck for someone else to find and assist. But when all that is said there still remains the question: Why did he do it? Why did he kill her? He certainly made a good job of hiding the body after he had done it. He was just unfortunate that it was found for there was nothing to connect him with her disappearance.

It is part of the nightmare of Norfolk that there are so many people around who are perfectly normal and respectable on the surface and have the ability to bury not just their victims but their own consciences so they do not get caught.

In a way, Heidi's parents were possibly lucky that they knew what had happened to her.

7

Exall

Beach Walk to Nowhere

Dark-haired Pamela Exall mounted her 175 cc Honda motor cycle and gave her parents a wave as she followed her brother Peter, aged seventeen, and his friend David at the start of their two week touring and camping holiday which was to take them from their homes in Fleet, Hampshire, to the Lake District and then on to Scotland and the Highlands before coming down the east coast, having a look at the Wash and Norfolk, and then going home.

For Pamela, twenty-one years old, it was the gap between graduating from law school and becoming an articled clerk with Berkshire county council. She was excited about the holiday and the future for she was a bright intelligent girl with everything to look forward to and live for.

A few days into the holiday the trio rang home, and then a few days later Pamela rang from Loch Ness to say they were having a lovely time, had not seen the monster, that everything was fine and that they would be home on Sunday just before the Bank Holiday. They had plenty to eat and their tents were ideal.

As the trio headed south the police in Norfolk were already at work at their regular but miserable task of identifying a body that had been dumped casually in Norfolk by a murderer who did not want his crime discovered. This was the body at Cockley Cley, the headless body, the identity of which has never been discovered (see Chapter 4).

The trio arrived in the King's Lynn area on Friday, 30 August 1974. They spent some time in the town, looking at the guildhall and the Tuesday market place and the shops before heading out towards the sea and a camp site for the night.

They made their way along the main road towards Hunstanton, the A149, past the royal estate at Sandringham, past Dersingham, until they took a left turn to go down towards the beach at Snettisham. It is just north of Bulldog and Peter Black Sands. They reached the camping site around 6.15 p.m. and put the tents up before going for a meal and a drink on the camp site. Similar camp sites can be found all round the Norfolk coast, tents mixing with caravans either on sites just for tents or caravans, some public and enormous (like the one from which Leoni Williams was so recently snatched at Great Yarmouth) or small and private.

The trio, relaxed and invigorated by their touring holiday which had been a roaring success, showered and changed for the evening. Then they went down to the club house for a meal and then just a few drinks and a chat about what they had done and what they had seen before they turned in for the night.

It was a beautiful August night when they came out of the club house. The moon was high in the sky, lighting up the area in a way which seems unique to Norfolk. It is as if there is a second coating of light to keep everything in place, a timelessness that only the most gifted can recreate but a feeling that when you see it, captures and excites you. Perhaps it was this that made Pamela decide to go for a walk, for it was still early, just 11.00 p.m. Perhaps it was because it was such a marvellous evening anyway and she fancied a walk along the golden sands that glistened in the moonlight as the sea lapped and turned with its eternal cry, out of sight but not out of hearing. The tide appeared to be out and the beach deserted.

Pamela went back to her tent and changed into her

walking shoes, leaving her other shoes neatly by her unrolled sleeping bag. She walked back to the club house to tell her brother and his friend what she was going to do and asked whether they wanted to join her for a late night stroll. They turned her down, explaining that they felt tired after their long journey, and she was quite happy about that. 'OK, see you later folks' she said, and turned and walked off to the beach.

It was the last time she was ever seen. She vanished in the way that people vanish in Norfolk, without trace, without leaving any clue as to what had happened, without anyone seeing her disappear in the sense that there was no witness who could say that she was heading for the sea or a car or transport.

Like April Fabb who rode off on her cycle, like Steven Newing who walked out of the house, Pamela just went. There was no expectation that she would go and never come back, there was no anticipation, no reason why she should, no clue that she met anyone who took her away or persuaded her to go, nothing to suggest that she had a secret so overpowering (or even trivial but vital to her) that would make her even consider taking her own life, for all the evidence was totally contradictory. She was like April and Steven (and the three are inevitably linked when the anniversaries come up or missing people are grouped together when a similar case occurs) in that she went off quite happy and within moments it was as if she had never existed. The North Sea has never returned her body, if in fact she went into the sea. If she had gone off with someone after a brainstorm which wiped out her memory, there has never been a hint that she is still alive. The brainstorm may never have altered and she may not know who she is, but this is conjecture of the highest level without evidence.

The next morning, the boys woke to the morning sun and went to wake Pamela up for breakfast. She was not in the tent. Inside was her sleeping bag still neatly rolled up, her kitbag containing her money, her cheque book, diary and keys, including the key for her motor cycle which was propped up outside the tent. She had obviously not come back and had been out all night.

Peter got on his motorbike and rode along the beach while his friend started walking round the camp site looking for her in the club house, calling outside the bath houses and toilets. Peter rode right along the beach, asking people if they had seen his pretty sister. No one had. All day they looked, all day that Saturday as people left for home, as newcomers arrived for the last week of the holiday season before work and school restarted. There was no sign of her. Frantic, they rang home to see if something had upset her and she had caught a train back to Hampshire, back home to her parents. They had not seen her, or heard from her since the happy call from Loch Ness six days before.

By late afternoon the boys were in despair and Peter went to the police station in King's Lynn and then to the hospital, but there was no sign of her. He rode back to the coast and went to Hunstanton police station to report her missing.

One can imagine the scene as he told the desk sergeant. The sergeant's heart must have sunk as he heard the details of a missing girl, the second in a fortnight in the county, just another in the long line that began with April Fabb. The sergeant took the details and then followed the routine procedure in these cases. Regional Headquarters in King's Lynn was told and they passed the information on to county headquarters in Norwich, nearly 50 miles away.

The searches started. Police with dogs searched all along the coastline in case she could have walked on and on and then fallen asleep exhausted and been taken ill while sleeping and be still sleeping there. A fit young girl could cover a long way on a moonlit night.

Farmers in the area were alerted and asked to look out for her in case she should be alive or dead in one of their fields, in case (although they did not say so) she had been murdered after being picked up on the beach and killed and her body dumped. Farmers harvested their sugar beet early to help the hunt.

Appeals were put out through the press, both local and national (because of the connection with April and Steven the reporters were there from the start), radio and television. They produced absolutely nothing.

Fishermen and other sailors were asked to look out for her. If she had gone into the sea, either because she wanted to or because she had done so by accident, it was more than likely her body would be brought back by the sea itself. It was not.

A clairvoyant was called in to help. He could not take the case any further than Pamela walking along the beach in the moonlight. There can be little doubt that as she did so she recalled her happy holiday and her future, the future that she was never to have. The dream when she left Kingston Polytechnic just four weeks before that she would have a great career in the law was never to be realized.

Her picture was shown everywhere in the days and weeks that followed her disappearance. There was no real lead and never has been.

If one looks at all the evidence, including her state of mind, her past life, her plans for the future, the circumstances that took her to Norfolk, what she had done before she got there, what she did while she was there, the happy afternoon, the pleasant convivial evening, the weather, the lure of a walk on the beach on a wonderful summer's evening, it is fair and reasonable to conclude that in her totally relaxed state of mind she did not notice the tide slipping in and, when she did, it was too late and she was cut off and drowned. It is the theory the police hold, and it is the most likely answer to the puzzle. No one can ever be sure, but it is likely and a more pleasant (if anything about death can be), solution than the theories of abduction and murder that still surround the disappearances of April and Steven.

8

Marymont

Wife Poisoner at USAF Base

Little America, the affectionate name that some give to the
United States Air Force base at RAF Sculthorpe, has been
just outside Fakenham and not far from the coast,
Hunstanton and the royal estate at Sandringham since the
Second World War. For a long time it was an important
strategic base for it was a nuclear base, though this was
officially denied. During this time various crimes and
events happened at the base. Two British electricians were
marched off at gunpoint accompanied by a stinging quote
from the then press officer who informed the newspapers
that the same thing would happen to the Queen of
England in similar circumstances. The circumstances were
never fully explained.

Then there were the two airmen who were held in open
custody on suspicion of bank robbery off base. One Bank
Holiday weekend they blew the base bank and stole tens
of thousands of dollars and cheques and drafts. They did a
good job, jamming the door back in place and bringing the
usual denials from the Americans that it was they who did
it. In those days the American Air Force had some
wonderful press officers for Third Air Force, pleasant men
who could tell you the most bare-faced lie without a blink
of shame on the orders of their masters, and become quite
indignant if you doubted their word. Only once did I find
them embarrassed.

A newspaper, long defunct, ran a story about drunken orgies at a nearby USAF base, just over the border into Suffolk, where officers of American, British and other nationalities went regularly to a house where girls employed by the Russians plied them with drink to extract secrets. The story in the paper – and it covered both front and back pages – went into detail but without specifically quoting anyone by name. It landed on the news desks in the other Fleet Street offices and nearly caused premature heart attacks. It had everything, and reporters were dispatched into the night tọ race to the base and find the Mata Haris who were doing this plying in exchange for top secrets, for they were secrets worth having: East Anglia (and Norfolk in particular) was the home of the A-bomb and the bombers who carried them, flying in rota twenty-four hours a day in case of Russian attack. Other reporters were on the phone to Ruislip where Third Air Force headquarters were, all demanding information. There was none to be had.

The Third Air Force press officers were genuinely baffled. They told all the reporters who called in a non-stop stream all night long (because the American press corps in London had been awoken to the story and US television was on its way to sleepy Suffolk) that they did not know anything about it. This was greeted with derision because the fame of the press officers in evading the truth and putting out bland statements which said that the facts were not true were legendary. The press officers insisted that the story was not true but the inquiring press did not believe them.

At the base the resident press officer, a regular captain who had been given the job as part of his career line, fended off all inquiries by referring them to Third Air Force. The truth was that Third Air Force was in a panic not matched until some years later when a drunk airman stole a Hercules C130 reconnaissance aircraft to impress his girl friend and flew off towards Europe and Russia, chased very quickly by some fighters who shot him down off the Channel Islands; the man was exceptionally drunk, so drunk in fact that he had been locked up earlier in the evening but released, and he was not permitted to fly. The shooting down was officially denied but a few days later aircraft were ball and chained to the concrete of the airfield to stop someone else stealing them.

The night wore on as reporters went round every pub, club and drinking venue in the area (and there were many) trying to find one lead that could put them on to the trail of these beautiful girls working for the Russians whose skills had now increased to sexual favours as well, as locals added to the information the paper had already given.

All night long Third Air Force denied the story. They had to because for once it was just not true. What had happened was that two young airmen from the RAF had been caught playing with each other in an air raid shelter and were facing court martial. One had apparently rung the paper in question and had told them about parties and the paper had sent down one of their ace reporters who had added a bit here, and spoken to others there who had told him this and that, and he had put it all together into a racy, spicy and extremely readable but implausible front page story. The only checkable fact was that the sign outside the base said that it was secret and that was proved by the picture the paper carried.

Back at Sculthorpe they had had other minor troubles (before the Suffolk affair) and the year of the A-bomb threat was also the year when an event happened that produced far more publicity of the kind the USAF did not approve.

The man involved was Master Sergeant Marcus Marymont, a happily married father of three (or so everyone thought) with a lovely wife called Helen. Marymont came from Hobbsville, California, was forty-three and a Korean veteran with thirteen medals. His wife came with him when he was posted to Norfolk in 1956.

In the spring of 1958 they put on a pantomime for charity at the base. Marcus directed the panto, *Dick Whittington*, driving his wife and family down to the theatre in his big red Buick, a car that was familiar as it was parked outside so often, (and outside other places, as we shall see) where his wife was the wardrobe mistress and also made the tea for the cast.

The American-style version of *Dick Whittington* was done with verve and pace but it was not a great success. It did, however, bring the Marymont family together after an unhappy Christmas because Marcus, known as Marc, had to be away at the Third Office base at High Wycombe, which meant the rest of the family were on their own. It was during the run of the panto, which brought in an audience from as far afield as Hunstanton, that Marc talked to a friend and told him his secret.

He had a girl and he was hopelessly in love. And he began to cry. He said that his wife was very nice and would be prepared to forgive him but his girl friend ...

It started in July two years before when the handsome American was on secondment to High Wycombe. One evening, riding round in his red Buick, the party loving, convivial master sergeant stopped at a club in Maidenhead for a drink. It was there that he spotted Cynthia, an attractive 23-year-old assistant in a chemist's shop, separated from her husband, on the verge of a divorce and expecting her first child. The juke box was playing 'You are Everywhere' and Marc Marymont, in civvies, went over to Cynthia and asked her to dance. It was a simple request but it led to murder and an ordeal for the girl that she will never forget.

He ran Cynthia and her mother home in his shiny red Buick and later called to see her. Once became twice and then three times and then more often, and when she was in hospital having her baby son he came to visit her, unaware that she was in fact having a child. It was then that he told her he loved her and sent her a huge bouquet of carnations telling her to get well soon. From then on the love affair progressed rapidly. It was based on a lie. He said that he was married but getting divorced and his wife and family were in America because she did not want to travel with him while he was serving abroad. The truth was that they were only 130 miles away at the bomber base in windswept Norfolk.

Marc spent every weekend he could at Cynthia's home,

telling his wife that he had to be on detachment to High Wycombe. He promised to marry Cynthia, twenty years his junior, just as soon as his divorce came through. For their first Christmas together he gave her a grey lambswool stole. Then he gave her a sapphire and diamond ring as a token of their love. She wore it on her wedding ring finger. They wrote letters to each other, dozens of letters, all of which were to become evidence in a trial where Cynthia had to give evidence for two days. They made love, they became like husband and wife, they looked forward to the day when they would marry, they pledged their eternal love for each other. And as he made love, and as he loved, Marc Marymont was planning to get rid of his wife, not by divorce, but by murder: by poisoning her.

As the affair became more intense Helen Marymont, who had been in England for over two years, became slightly suspicious that her husband had another woman. She told a friend who commented that she looked happier that things were all right because she had written down everything she wanted to say to her husband and handed it to him. His reaction was to roar with laughter and put his arm round her and say 'Of course there is nobody else.' He told a good lie.

He had been to a chemist's shop in the town where Cynthia lived and asked if they kept arsenic. Told that they did but that he would need a permit to buy it he nodded and walked out. He had also been into the base laboratory and inspected the jars which contained arsenic and asked whether they were ever locked up. He told the cleaner: 'It would never do to take a lot of that.'

Mrs Marymont began to suffer from stomach troubles in the spring of 1958. On the evening of 8 June 1958, a fortnight after her husband had tried to buy arsenic in Maidenhead, she sat down for dinner at a friend's home. There were ten guests around the table. The next day she died in the base hospital, but none of the other nine guests, including her husband, suffered any after-effects.

Mrs Marymont definitely did. She was ill throughout the night and her husband went to the duty doctor and got medicine. It made no difference. She died far from her home in California so that her husband could marry an English girl.

When she was admitted to hospital she was almost dead. The doctor in charge considered poisoning and Marc Marymont told him that his wife had been ill in a similar way – but not so seriously – over the past year, and six weeks before she had been very ill. This would tie in with the findings of Mr Lewis Nickolls, director of the Scotland Yard laboratory, who told the court when the case came to trial that she had had a large dose of arsenic shortly before her death and also another anything up to a month or so before that.

The duty doctor at the base hospital questioned the husband about his wife's condition and then, to the doctor's astonishment, the master sergeant began to talk about his sex problems with his wife. The doctor told the court later: 'I felt at the time it was extraordinary.' After she died Marymont patted the doctor on the shoulder and said that he knew he was upset.

It was five weeks before he was arrested on two charges on which he faced a court martial at the USAF base at Denham, Bucks, in December 1958. He denied murdering his 43-year-old wife, a charge which could carry the death penalty, and also, as a married man, denied that he did 'wrongfully have sexual intercourse' with Cynthia, a woman not his wife, on various occasions between 20 December 1956 and 31 May 1958. Making love to his mistress was against Air Force law.

The prosecution said that he poisoned his wife because he was in love with another woman. The prosecutor said: 'This affair was not of the common variety but had gone on for two years to the point that marriage had been discussed in detail. The love was so overwhelming that Marymont spent nearly every other weekend with this woman and even spent Christmas in 1957 away from his wife and children.'

After she died Marc at first agreed to a post mortem but later withdrew his permission on the grounds that the children would not like their mother being cut up.

When she died an American doctor thought it might be arsenic poisoning but he was told that he had been reading too many mystery magazines and his theory was dismissed. But as the weeks went on officials became suspicious and eventually organs were sent to Scotland Yard.

The fourteen officers trying the case, in a building which was once the Denham film studios but was now a USAF supply depot, heard from the Maidenhead chemist how Marymont came into his shop asking about arsenic. They also heard from a neighbour of Mrs Marymont who said that the dead woman was making plans to go on a shopping spree and even getting ready for Christmas. She was also planning the family holiday in Scotland. She also said that at the fatal dinner – a birthday party – Helen was very happy. After Mrs Marymont's death, the neighbour went on, she met Marc in the club and he was crying because somebody had said that he had poisoned Helen because he had thrown a medicine bottle away.

Then Dr Francis Camps, the expert British Home Office pathologist, told the court that the evidence showed that Mrs Marymont died from arsenic poisoning but he had no way of knowing whether it was rat poison or whether it was self inflicted.

Another neighbour told how Helen, a religious and good woman who was an excellent mother devoted to her family, had said that she was getting fed up and blaming the Air Force for coming between her and her husband, but when she had suggested to him that she went with him on temporary duty he had said that he would be working all the time and she would be on her own.

Yet another neighbour said that Helen had told her 'I will see him dead in hell before I break my family up' and told another that if the family did not go back to the States soon she would go back in a box.

Her husband began his evidence by denying absolutely that he had ever bought arsenic, or that he had ever administered it to his wife. It is a statement that he has made constantly over the years and one from which he has never wavered.

He agreed that he was in love with Cynthia but not deeply in love. He admitted having a sexual relationship with her and that they had discussed marriage. He had given Cynthia presents, yes, he said, a coat – sent by mistake to Mrs Marymont – a ring, a wrap, even underwrote her television set even though his own family did not have one. (That was because his wife was opposed to it.) They had dinner at Claridge's, but he was also in debt, although meeting his commitments, even though he had to borrow to pay his telephone bill.

He said he loved his family but admitted he had spent Christmas with Cynthia instead of them. He said that his wife had found a letter which seemed to clarify the situation. His wife was determined to keep the family together and before there was any break up they should try to work the problem out.

But he agreed with the statement that if there had not been a hitch he would have married Cynthia and had already said that he would adopt her son on condition that they married.

Yes, he said, he had been to see Cynthia five days after his wife's death, and his children did not seem greatly upset about the death. It was Cynthia who told the court martial about the visit. Cynthia was in the witness box for two days, long days when her intimate life was exposed before foreigners in a way that does not happen under the British judicial system but is part and parcel of the American one, both in civilian and military life. From time to time she broke down, particularly when she was made to read dozens of the letters she had written to the master sergeant during his double life. Then they were handed to the board of fourteen officers, all of whom read them. At one point Cynthia broke down and wept and there was an adjournment, and the prosecuting attorney walked over to the witness he was examining, offered her a cigarette and lit it for her. Not the British way.

But Cynthia, dressed in black except for the grey fur stole that her lover had given her, stood up well and during her long examination revealed what he had said on the day he came to tell her that his wife had died.

'I said "in America" and he said no "in England". I said "but you told me you were divorced" and he said "yes I know".'

Then, she said, he added: 'I am awfully sorry.'

The shock to the young mother, anticipating marrying her handsome lover with the shiny red Buick that was often parked outside her home in Maidenhead, parked so often that it became a joke with the neighbours, must have been intense. But it did not alter her love or her wish to marry him, not for many years.

She gave evidence before Marc in the old film studio where human drama was being played out in a much more dramatic form than any films that had been made on the set. She sat alone in the centre of the room while she was questioned, while the love letters were handed round. She told how they first met in 1956, how they met once or twice a month, she thinking that he was divorced, he telling her that or leading her to believe it, how they discussed marriage in 1957 and how he gave her a ring. 'Was it an engagement ring?' asked the prosecuting officer. She studied her hands and her long brightly painted red finger nails and said that it could not be an engagement ring because she was married at the time. She was asked about the gifts that Marymont gave her, the fur for instance. 'I'll show you if you like' she said, holding up the one she had brought with her.

Marc was with her over Christmas 1957, she thinking that his wife and family were in the States, although that did not matter to the two lovers. One knew where they were, the other did not care because she was so happy.

Five days after Mrs Marymont died, Marymont came to her house. It was the first time she had seen him since her birthday on 23 May and the two days that followed the occasion. He had taken her to Claridge's to celebrate on 24 May, not many days before the fateful birthday party in Norfolk when, somehow, Helen Marymont dined and managed to eat a killer dose of arsenic.

After his wife's death Marc spent two days with his mistress in their love-nest in Maidenhead. It was strong, gripping information, important pieces in the prosecution case to show that this was a man who killed to find happiness with another woman.

Cynthia revealed the plans that she and the man she loved had made for the future when her divorce came through. She knew all about his family and children (apart from the fact that his wife was in England, believing that she had a happy marriage), how they would marry then and where he was she would be too.

That was the evidence before the panel of officers went to decide the fate of the serviceman who had never had a blemish on a career that included war service in Japan and Korea and who had the Soldier's Medal for saving a man's life on a blazing ship in Alaska during the early days of American participation in the Second World War. Did he really kill his wife?

The prosecuting captain had no doubt. Marymont, he said, was a cool, calculating egotist who had the 'diabolical thought' of feeding small amounts of arsenic to his wife to give the impression that she was suffering from a normal illness when he decided to get rid of her.

'The type of person who would commit this type of crime has to be cool, calculating and intelligent. If Marymont does not fit that description no one does.'

The lover, former smooth-talking radio announcer, sat with his head in his hands. He had reason to, for the prosecutor went relentlessly on:

'We know he spent Christmas with Cynthia away from his wife and children. Any man who would leave three children at Christmas, which is the children's time, is cool, calculating and without scruples. He is a man who would do anything.'

On his desk at the base were the letters that went between him and Cynthia. There had been no attempt to hide them, the prosecutor said, and it was easy to see why. Marymont, he declared, was an egotist rapidly approaching middle age, and here he had a young girl in her twenties 'madly in love with him'. He went on scathingly: 'At no time did he expect his wife's death to appear as anything but a natural death. We see no reason why he should not discuss Cynthia with his friends. It was better if it was known he had a girl friend before his wife died than suddenly to introduce one after her death.'

The prosecutor declared that as a witness Marymont was the coolest and the calmest. 'He has lived with this thing and he knew exactly what he was going to say. This man decided he had to dispose of his wife. She was sick normally and under the care of a doctor. Enter the diabolical thought: what kind of poison would give symptons which would give the impression that it was really severe bouts of her normal illness? He tried a small dose of arsenic but it doesn't work. In May he tries another dose. It almost works but she recovers from that. He waits until June and tries again.'

If the prosecutor is right, he is painting a terrible scenario. The lover is bedding the mistress while at the same time trying to kill, trying to murder in the coldest of bloods by poison, the most awful way of killing, particularly one whom you loved, his wife.

'He goes to the hospital for some medicine and dumps that dose of arsenic into that medicine. The medicine given to her to make her better makes her worse.'

And he accused the lover of delaying taking his wife to hospital so that there was no mistake. He declared:

'He wanted to make sure Mrs Marymont did not send one of the children for the doctor, he had failed twice before. Now he was going to supervise the job himself and make sure it went through.'

It was a terrible portrait he sketched of this war hero. Where had he got the poison? Was it really Mrs Marymont's liver that was examined? Those were two questions the Board of Officers would have to consider when deliberating their verdict. But the prosecutor left them in no doubt as to the case the state was pursuing. He said that everything in the master sergeant's life was coming to a head; he stood the chance of losing the girl he loved unless his wife was out of the way, and the only way of ensuring that was to kill her. He would win his freedom by poisoning her.

Not so, the defence insisted. The major, leading the team, said:

'It has not been proved that death could only have been caused by Marymont. The probability of suicide or accident is just as great, if not greater, than murder. The only thing we have here is purely conjecture, speculation and suspicion.

'If that is enough to convict a man of the most serious crime he could be charged with we need to pray for the whole judicial system.

'It is anybody's guess whose liver was analysed by Dr Nickolls and it is on this liver that the prosecution findings have been based.'

There was doubt in the evidence that the officers had heard about whose liver from the hospital it was on which Mr Nickolls performed his tests. The same doubt was cast on where the arsenic came from and whether Helen Marymont took it herself because she had found out about her husband's young mistress and decided to take the easy (or hard) way out.

The defence major talked of the affair. It was not any great and glowing romance, he said. It was just a sordid little romance of the kind that breaks up thousands of families every year. 'But,' he insisted 'this is not the type of love affair that drives a man to murder.'

And the letters, those hundreds of laboriously written words between a younger woman desperately in love with a man twenty years her senior, what of those? Were they passionate, throbbing words that could turn a man to murder to keep the woman he loved? No, no, no, said the defence. 'The letters that have been paraded before you show a marked cooling in the affections of Cynthia towards the sergeant. They were ordinary letters from people who had no particular affection for each other.

'I would submit that if you have a girl friend, and that is motive enough to convict a man of murder, then God help the greatest proportion of our society because we know that this thing does exist day in day out and it certainly does not create motives in every instance nor in this instance, for murder.'

It was a fine balance. The prosecution said that the lover had obtained poison and fed it to his wife and killed her to retain his beloved. The defence said there was no proof that he had done so: it was all circumstantial evidence and suspicion.

The trial had lasted nine days, there had been sixty-one witnesses and more than one hundred exhibits.

It was six days before Christmas and both Marymont and Cynthia must have ruefully remembered the previous Christmas when they were so blissfully happy, he with a younger woman, she thinking that he was on the verge of divorce and she on the verge of a new and happy marriage after one unsuccessful one.

The officers took five hours to consider their verdict. It was guilty as charged on both counts. The lover, the father, stood absolutely still, stunned. It was 10.05 p.m. and he had left his cup of coffee when he was called to face the board. He never went back to the coffee.

The verdict was reached with a two-thirds majority, and all that remained was sentence to be fixed. There was nothing hurried about that, although Marymont faced death. The court adjourned until 9.00 a.m.

On 19 December they were all back in the former film studios. It would need a unanimous verdict of all the officers to declare the death sentence. Instead they voted by more than a two-thirds majority to lock him up for life (and in the United States that can mean what it says, unlike Britain where 'life' can mean anything from two years to twenty, if the judge has not made a recommendation for a minimum number of years to be served).

Marymont had to wait sixteen hours to hear whether he would live or die. At least he knew ahead what could happen. His wife did not.

The president of the court, Colonel Albert Snider, told the poisoner (who was going to have a very long time to think about what he had done – although he still strenuously denied it):

'It is my duty as president of this court to inform you that the court in closed session and upon secret written ballots, three of the members present at the time the vote was taken concurring, sentences you to be dishonourably discharged from the Service, forfeit all pay and allowances and be confined to hard labour for the term of your natural life.'

The sting was in the tail, and Master Sergeant Marc Marymont, who was known as a man who did good works for the boy and girl scouts with his wife, now deceased and out of the way, saluted and went back to the table where he sat with his counsel.

After the court was adjourned he did an American act. He went to the Board of Officers who had just taken away his freedom forever to thank them for 'their fair jurisdiction on the facts in their minds'. It is not an action that has ever happened in a British court. No defendant who has been sentenced to life goes up and shakes the hand of the judge who has handed it down.

As he was taken into an office to await going back to the USAF stockade at Bushey, where he would be held before going back to the States for appeals and then, if they were turned down, to serve his sentence in the stockade at Leavenworth, Kansas, the reporters were vying to get an interview with him. His mistress, the girl he wanted to marry, had already been bought up, and in the articles ghosted for her she told how he was the love of her life and how she would wait and stand by him.

But he had not spoken, and in the event he spoke to only one reporter, Brian Park of the *Daily Express*, who had had the ingenuity to hand two letters to Marymont's defending counsel, one saying 'congratulations' and to be handed to him if he was acquitted, requesting an interview. Letter B was the one that said 'commiserations' if he was convicted and sentenced and requesting an interview to put the guilty man's side. The defending officer thought it was all a bit cold blooded (not that the murder had been anything other) but did as he was asked and it did the trick.

It was fine journalistic enterprise but Marymont only said what one would have expected from a man who had protested his innocence all the way through the investigation and the trial. He said:

'Every single thing I said in the court was the truth. I did not murder my wife and I will maintain my innocence forever. I will appeal.

'The court martial was just and fair and the court members acted according to their own consciences.'

He said of the woman whom he loved and who was the centre of the trial: 'Meeting her was the turning point of my life. It was a turning point I would rather have avoided. I have not seen her or heard anything from her. If she wants to write that's up to her.'

He was upset at the loss of his service life for it had been his life for twenty years.

Then he said goodbye to his mother Gertrude, who had flown over from California to be with her only child during his trial, and his son, before going to the stockade still insisting that he had done everything a husband could do for his wife and certainly not killed her.

Brian Park kept in touch with Marymont. Two years later he went to see him in Leavenworth, Kansas, where the former sergeant was able to tell him that the American Air Force had granted him a review of his trial. The Court of Military Appeals had the power to order a retrial or quash the original sentence. And the man who was there because of his love for another woman, a woman he still wanted to marry, a woman with whom he was not allowed to communicate because she still had not been divorced but who sent the message that she still loved him, that he was never out of her thoughts and that she would marry him there and now, was sure that because he had not had a fair trial he would succeed.

His final words at the end of the interview were: 'Tell Cynthia I love her and I'll be back one day.' It was not to be. His case was reviewed and his sentence reduced to thirty-five years and the charge of adultery dismissed. He was let out long before he served anything like that. He was released on parole after nine years and became a radio announcer and disc jockey in Arkansas.

But Cynthia did not wait. In 1964 her husband obtained a divorce on the grounds of her adultery with Marymont. She had promised to wait and had sworn eternal love. He had proposed to her by letter during the first year of his sentence and she had accepted. Time dragged heavily and it was too long for a young girl, twenty years younger than her lover. She regarded the years of waiting as hopeless; met another man and married him. Marymont was shattered when he heard. He said that the two years that he had had with her were the happiest of his life.

Then he came out of prison and started a new life himself. His plea for a new trial never came to anything. He just went on living over 3,000 miles from the piece of Norfolk where he is recorded as having poisoned his wife for love of another.

Many kill their wives for a variety of reasons but mainly because of another woman. Most do it with their hands or a ligature or a knife or a gun. Arsenic is very rare and the most bone chilling in its cruelty and length of time to finish off the once-loved partner.

Marymont was prepared to do this, making love to his new girl as the old one died in agony over the weeks, the prosecution declared. Marymont said he did not do it. His wife never had the chance to say either way because throughout her illness caused by the poisoning she did not know what was happening to her.

No one will ever be sure. Or will there be one who will be?

9

Bushell

Three Dead Then Murder

To misquote Oscar Wilde: to lose one child is a misfortune, to lose two is carelessness. Margaret Bushell lost four. Three were by accident but the fourth was different, as we shall see. The extraordinary thing was that she was a perfectly normal woman, a caring, loving mother, hard working, gentle, kind, keeping a clean loving home for her husband and the many children in their council house home in Downham Market.

Downham Market is what its name implies, a market town standing above the surrounding fens on the banks of the Ouse, 12 miles south of Kings Lynn. It was an important centre in Roman times, and the A1122 from Norwich to Peterborough, the north and the Midlands, and the A10 from Kings Lynn to Ely, Cambridge and London still cross there, confirming this fact. Nowadays it is a busy small town with its weekly market.

Mrs Bushell moved to Norfolk in 1953 from her native Manchester after her first marriage ended in divorce. She had two children by her first marriage, a daughter, Denise, and a son, Terry, now both in early middle age. She became housekeeper to a man twenty-one years older than herself, Sidney Bushell, a railway bill poster. After a short time they married and had five children.

In March 1958, tragedy struck the happy home. Cheryl Diana, aged three, was found face down in the bath. It contained 6 inches of water which was mixed with a strong bleach. It happened while her mother had popped next door for some potatoes. When she returned she found the toddler. She told the coroner at the inquest that she found some paper in the bath and the little girl might have lost her balance and fallen in as she tried to retrieve it.

The coroner was Arthur Bantoft, the Norfolk coroner and a solicitor. It was the first time he had met the Bushells but it was not to be the last. Their family doctor, a woman, told him that Margaret and Sidney were excellent parents and the coroner expressed his sympathy and returned a verdict of accidental death.

It was only six weeks later that tragedy hit the neat council house again. Stephen, their eldest child, was five that day. His mother made him a special treat for his supper, his favourite of bread and butter sandwiches spread with tomato ketchup. He went up to bed a happy little boy. During the night he somehow climbed out of his bedroom window and crashed 12 feet to the concrete path below, where he was found at 6.15 a.m. with a broken neck and spinal injuries.

At the inquest the same people assembled again – the coroner, the lady doctor, the Bushells, Sid holding his broken-hearted wife's hand.

She told Mr Bantoft: 'Stephen suffered from nightmares. He used to sleepwalk. The window was slightly open but it was quite safe as it was screwed down but somehow while he was asleep he must have got the screw out and the window open.'

The doctor confirmed that the Bushells had told her about the little boy's sleepwalking and the coroner returned a verdict of death by misadventure.

There was a great deal of genuine – and genuinely deserved – sympathy in the town for the Bushell family. Everyone could feel for them for such an awful tragedy to happen, not just once, but twice. But life had to go on, not just for people who would have been only too happy to help if they could have done, but also for the Bushells and their two other children who were still alive.

Twenty months later, in January 1960, another was dead. This time it was Timothy, aged three, and he drowned in the family clothes boiler, head down in just 7 inches of water. His father was at home, watching television on the Saturday afternoon with his baby daughter Jane on his knee looking at the racing. For four hours he did not check where young Timothy was and it was not until his mother came home from work, making the tea at a local hotel, that she found him. The same lady doctor came to certify him dead.

It was the second child they had lost by drowning, and this time the coroner commented that it was extraordinary that two should have died from falling in water and incredible that the mother should have left it in a boiler, the first death having happened from water left in the bath, knowing that the toddler went into the wash house.

The coroner heard that Timothy was last seen around 2.00 p.m. on the Saturday and that his father never moved from the television to look for him. The coroner said: 'He was not really worrying where the boy was. I think most parents would go round to the next door neighbour and say "Is Timothy here?" but Mr Bushell does nothing about it, not even when daylight has turned to darkness. Well, I cannot comment on it, but I simply draw attention to the evidence given to me.'

He had words for the mother too after she told him that she had put water in the boiler ready to wash some nappies the next day. She explained that because the tap had leaked her husband had fixed it two years before, so that now the tap could not be used at all; but she admitted that she had never asked her husband to have it properly repaired.

The coroner said: 'It never seems to dawn on either Mr or Mrs Bushell the danger of water. Nothing is done about the leaking tap except it is bunged up and Mrs Bushell just puts the water in.'

Then he turned to the fact that two other children of theirs had died. He said, returning a verdict of accidental death: 'The rather extraordinary thing is that Cheryl's death was also the result of falling in water which was in the bath. It seems incredible to me that having lost one child in that way the mother should leave water in a boiler knowing that the child goes into the wash house frequently.'

The Bushells went back to their semi and tongues began to wag, suggesting not that the deaths were anything more than a horrible coincidence of bad luck, all thoroughly investigated by the police, but that the Bushells were not really fit to be in charge of children. Losing three was more than ordinary misfortune, the locals said, and although they felt deeply for the poor parents they believed they should have taken more care because with more care two certainly could have been avoided.

The Bushells did not agree. Sid was quite outspoken about it. He said: 'We must be one of the unluckiest families in the country. I think there's a jinx on us or on this house.'

His wife agreed: 'We've never had anything but bad luck since we moved here seven years ago. We are not bad parents. We have always fed and clothed the children well, not letting them run around hungry and in rags like some people do.'

Her husband added: 'A few nasty-minded people have tried to make a scandal out of us losing three children. But a lot of kind people have written to us expressing sympathy and given us a lot of old fashioned superstitious hints on how to change our luck. But the first thing we are going to do is to move away from this house with all its unhappy memories. Perhaps that will change our luck. We can't stand another tragedy in this family.'

They did not move away. Their luck did not change. There were two more tragedies, not just one.

Five years later they had another child, Simon. Three years after that Margaret's husband died of cancer and she was left to look after their two children, Jane and Simon (their older two by her first marriage were grown up and had left home).

Simon was the apple of her eye and she spoilt him. She loved him and his sister and could not do more for them, going out to work long hours in local pubs or as a receptionist.

There was only one problem and that was Simon's annoying habits. They were those that afflict many boys: blinking his eyes, twitching his nose, kicking his legs as he walked. Then he started shaking his head, which annoyed his mother even more. She saw the doctor who told her not to worry because many boys of his age behaved in the same way. But Mrs Bushell, she of the rare smile, could not accept it. It got on top of her, and in an attempt to stop Simon she gave him tranquillizers and sleeping pills prescribed for her.

On Christmas Day, 1972, Simon, then aged seven, opened his presents and the day passed with his mother becoming more and more upset by the little boy's nose twitching. She was sure he was doing it deliberately. At 2.00 a.m. on Boxing Day the phone rang in the local police station. It was Mrs Bushell and she had a short but chilling message to give.

'I have killed my little boy' she said.

The police went round to the house in Retreat Estate to investigate the death of the fourth Bushell child to die in strange circumstances, except that this time there was no accident, no death by misadventure. It was straightforward murder.

Mrs Bushell made no bones about it, telling the police four times that she had killed the boy and making a statement to that effect. She was taken from her home to the courthouse at King's Lynn, where she had been three times before with her now dead husband to give evidence on the deaths of three earlier occasions; she was sent on remand in custody to await her trial in the old Castle Assize courtroom in Norwich.

She looked so placid and quiet and normal when she came up into the dock in May to plead not guilty to the murder of Simon. The jury, which included a pregnant young woman, were sworn in. They had no idea about the history of the Bushell family and no one was going to tell them. The fact that three children had died accidentally was not germane to the case and would certainly have been prejudicial because they would start wondering whether in fact the deaths were by accident, whether there had been a hand to push a little girl in the bath, a boy out of the window, another little boy in the washing boiler in the outhouse. It would only be human nature to wonder that. The police had investigated each death all those years back. The coroner had wondered but had found it definitely was not true, just a sad coincidence that no one could recall ever happening to any other family in Britain. The neighbours and the people of Norfolk knew all about the deaths because they had been covered in greater and greater detail as the numbers increased, and most of those who read the coverage must have had thoughts. It was a natural thing to consider. But the verdicts showed that there was no truth in such thoughts.

What this jury knew was that this 49-year-old widow was sitting quietly dressed as if she was just going to her job as a hotel receptionist or to work behind the bar in one of the small town's hotels and that she said she had not murdered her youngest son, her only son by her dead second husband.

Mr David Hunter, QC, outlined the facts to them. The details relied very much on what Mrs Bushell told the police, that Simon's little habits finally became too much for her. In the statement she made to the police she described them. She said: 'It started when he began blinking his eyes, wiping and twitching his nose for no reason and kicking his legs with his heels as he walked. He kept this up for several weeks and it worked me up. Then he started shaking his head and that put the top hat on it. I was worried that the children at school might make fun of him because of these habits.'

She saw the doctor and he told her not to worry but she started giving him the pills the doctor had prescribed for her and she gave him some on Christmas night. But, her statement went on: 'After giving him the sleeping tablets I started to go downstairs and he began shouting. Everything seemed to get on top of me and I had reached the end of my tether.'

The little boy had got out of bed and she had tucked him in and then he started shouting as she went downstairs. It was after midnight and she had had enough. Those who knew the family history could understand that she must be on edge with the terrible weight of the tragedies in the past. Each day must have been hard with those memories in her mind, never going away. And now this little boy, with his irritating habits that had wound her up in the weeks before Christmas, was shouting in the early hours of Boxing Day and she had had enough.

She told the police in her statement: 'He was still shouting so I went upstairs grabbed a pillow and held it over his face for a few minutes. He did not make any more noise. I thought he was dead when I took it off his face.'

Four times she confessed in those early hours. First she told her lady doctor, a different one to the doctor who had been in attendance for the first three deaths, although she still lived in the town after retiring. Mrs Bushell said: 'I have killed my little boy.'

Then she rang Norwich police station and told the duty constable: 'I have just killed my son. He was seven years old.' Then she twice confessed to Detective Chief Inspector Charles Nourse, who went to the house where he found Simon in bed with two pillows over his face. He was obviously dead.

Mr Hunter told the jury that there was no complaint about Mrs Bushell as a mother. She was, he said, over-protective and indulgent towards him. 'She was possibly over-concerned about his little habits.'

This was confirmed by her other son, Simon's step-brother Terry. He gave evidence and told the jury: 'Mum worshipped Simon. She never slapped him and he never wanted for anything. He was a spoiled child.'

But Mr Hunter had also to tell them the unpalatable truth. He said that by committing the murder she was a very wicked woman and said: 'It is an unpleasant story with only one answer – she intended to do what she did and was aware of the inevitability of the consequences.'

There was no dispute over what the police said Mrs Bushell told them. She was not denying that. So just said that she did not mean to murder her son. She explained: 'On Christmas night I was reading a book but could not concentrate.' Throughout the day Simon was deliberately annoying her by twitching his nose, she thought.

'He was in need of some treatment. If I could have taken him to the doctors I would have done so. But this was Christmas and it all got too much for me. I just did not know what had happened.'

In the early hours of Boxing Day, soon after midnight, she heard him moving about upstairs, so she climbed the stairs to his bedroom. She said – and the whole court was still and silent so that they could hear every word – 'I seemed to be in a dream, a haze. Everything seemed to be going round. I felt funny and everything seemed to be a long way off. There were all kinds of flashing coloured lights in front of my eyes, my ears were pumping and everything was a cotton wool world.'

The silence was uncanny. She went on in her soft, friendly voice, matter of fact although only like that to cover her deep emotion: 'I only put a pillow over his face to frighten him. If I had realized I was hurting him I would not have done it as I loved him so much. I did not know what I was doing. I remember picking a pillow up. I remember putting it on Simon's face. For a second I could not see anything but I knew I was doing wrong but I did not know what I was doing wrong. I just wanted to frighten him, to stop him making a noise. Suddenly I was looking at his hand and it just dropped. It had only taken a second.'

But what had led up to this act? 'It all began when he began carrying a handkerchief in his hand and wiping his nose for no reason at all.' She went to the doctor to tell him about her son's habits and her anxiety and she was given sleeping tablets.

'I gave some to Simon to calm him down' she said. They clearly did not work.

Having heard all the evidence, the judge summed up to the jury and made one obvious point. He said: 'You may find at the very minimum she has committed the offence of manslaughter.'

The judge was Mr Justice Caulfield who was later to win international fame as the judge who described Jeffrey Archer's wife Mary as radiant, elegant and fragrant. In

1973 he was a judge on circuit and a pleasant, well-liked man who showed mercy and treated people, whether defendants, the Bar or the press, with consideration. In the old court at Norwich there was not a great deal of room for the press and he was known to invite the overspill to sit up on the bench with him. He also allowed the press – but no one else – to come and go as they pleased while witnesses were giving evidence, realizing that they had deadlines to meet.

He also realized the great strain of giving evidence by people being tried for crimes of passion or domestic murder, people who would not otherwise be in front of a judge. Once at Ipswich a middle-aged man who had killed his menopausal wife after another spate of nagging was asked, in cross-examination, about a lady friend he had. The prosecutor was ready to accuse him, but as he was about to frame the vital question Mr Justice Caulfield stopped him. Instead of the grilling he was about to get, the defendant was offered a cup of tea for, said the judge, it was the kind of day when everyone needed a break for a cup of tea. He suggested that one of the lady ushers at Ipswich might be a good tea maker but she had to tell him that there were no facilities, just a machine.

The Bushell jury were out for some time and in the end the judge had to declare that he would accept a majority verdict. They returned a guilty of murder by eleven to one. The pregnant juror was crying. Perhaps she could not believe that a mother could kill her child. No one was to know; but I wonder what she thought the next day when she read in the papers about the accidental deaths of the three other children.

The judge did not waste words. Everyone felt for the sad-faced woman in the dock. There was only one sentence, one of life imprisonment, and he passed it quickly, saying 'I do not think it appropriate that I should pass any comment.' Mrs Bushell looked at him and then went passively away with the two women prison officers. She did not seem to understand or, if she did, she was not going to show it.

The next morning the front pages of the tabloids were

covered with the story of the three previous accidents and photographs of the mother and the little boy she had killed. Even the more serious papers gave a large amount of space to the story and the background. It was the major talking point of the day in the cafés and clubs, restaurants and pubs. What had really happened to those other children? There was massive speculation, but no proof either way. One positive factor was that she had not touched her two children by her first marriage. They had nothing but good to say of her.

Terry, then twenty-seven, said: 'My mother was always very good to me when I was a boy. She was a good mum, always working hard, always on the go. She loved any little baby. It was a tremendous shock to me when I was told that Simon was dead. She doted on him, spoilt and pampered him. He got his own way a lot because she was so soft with him.'

He was only twelve and thirteen when the other three, his step-brothers and sister, died but he remembered being very upset. He said: 'My mother was on sedatives when it all happened. She was terrifically upset but she seemed to get over it. The police investigated at the time. The deaths were put down as accidents. It was accepted, it was just one of those things.'

He talked too about Christmas Day when he had gone over with his wife and baby and how his mother played with the baby, making her laugh as she bumped her up and down on her knee. As she did so Simon played happily with his toys.

It might have been just one of those things back in 1959 and 1960, but with the murder added to make the total of dead children four, there were bound to be calls for further investigation, another look at the past. They came from two Norfolk MPs – Paul Hawkins, Tory MP for south-west Norfolk in whose constituency Mrs Bushell lived, then a government whip, now Sir Paul, and Dr Tom Stuttaford, Tory MP for Norwich south.

Dr Stuttaford said that he was going to talk to Mr Hawkins about the desirability of raising the matter with the Home Secretary, who was then Robert Carr, now Lord

Carr. The doctor said: 'One wonders how it was that Simon Bushell who, on his mother's own admission, was showing signs of psychiatric disturbance was allowed to remain in the house where there had been such a terrible series of tragic deaths pointing at least to a remarkable degree of accident proneness.'

At the same time Norfolk police announced there were no grounds for reopening inquiries, and the coroner who had dealt with the first three deaths said that he stood by his verdicts. They were, he said, the right verdicts following police evidence.

All three children had been cremated. There was no post mortem in the first two cases but the cause of death when Tim died in the boiler was death by drowning.

Added to those who spoke out was the then director of social services for Norfolk who said that after the death of Tim, the third child, the children's officer in 1960 wrote to the NSPCC and the police saying the social services were concerned about what had happened. An NSPCC officer made visits to the house and spoke to doctors, neighbours and others who knew the family, and the evidence was that the other children were much-loved, well-nourished and well-clothed.

The director said: 'Since that time nothing has been brought to our attention to cause us any anxiety about the way the children were being looked after.'

The only remaining child at home, Jane, aged fifteen, was sent to a foster home and then to foster parents. She was allowed to go to see her mother whenever she wanted.

Mr Hawkins did indeed press his request for an inquiry and the Home Secretary ordered one. It was carried out by a senior Norfolk police officer who had had nothing to do with the earlier inquiries. His report said what was already known: that each case was carefully investigated at the time but that the inquiries showed that they were just accidents to an unlucky family.

In August the result of that inquiry was announced and that was the end of the Bushell case except that she had to serve her sentence and life had to go on for the three who survived.

The chances of such a run of death by disaster happening three times are beyond mathematical probability. For a fourth (and this time by the hand of a mother who has already had to suffer three accidents within fourteen months) to occur is – literally – unbelievable. But it happened.

10

Drinkwater

Doctor Death and the Porno Pics

Peter Drinkwater was born with a medical spoon in his mouth. His father was a successful doctor and the boy was handsome, talented and good at sport. His future stretched out before him like a golden rug.

He went to Gresham's School in Norfolk (where he shares the unpleasant fact that he and five-times killer Jeremy Bamber are both old boys) and learnt to play hockey very well indeed. It stood him in good stead at Cambridge where he got his Blue and even a trial for England while at Magdalene College.

He studied medicine at St Bartholomew's Hospital in London and qualified in 1959. The good-looking young man joined the Army on a five-year commission in the Royal Army Medical Corps at the age of twenty-four and was posted overseas to Guyana and Germany. It was while on active service that the first signs of the flaw that was to cost him everything began to appear. He drank heavily but mixed his drink with a combination of amphetamines, a pep pill – alcohol cocktail that added spice to life but did not help him with his job. It was a mixture he had learnt about during his fourth year as a medical student, a lesson he could well have done without. The Army found out, he was reprimanded and then sent home.

When he came out of the Army he went into general

practice in Reading, married and seemed to settle down. By that time he had been warned by the Home Office about his future conduct after his behaviour had been reported to the Medical Drugs Committee.

The smiling, smooth young doctor was popular with his patients. But he was still in trouble with the authorities, being fined first for careless driving, then for dangerous driving. Then, early in 1971, he was fined £100 and banned from driving for three years after admitting causing the death by dangerous driving of a 72-year-old cyclist.

The doctor, then aged thirty-five, married with two children, appeared in the town where he practised, standing in the dock in the old Berkshire Assize court. The judge, Mr Justice Paull, heard how Drinkwater overtook another car in a built-up area at a speed between 55 and 60 mph and hit the old man, who was travelling correctly on his side of the road, head on. The cycle was dragged 40 yards down the road before Drinkwater stopped. He got out, walked back to the body, felt the old man's pulse and told witnesses: 'He's dead.' He drove off and it was not until thirty minutes later that he phoned the police. When a policeman called at his home he said: 'I knew he had died. I am only interested in the living, not the dead.'

The doctor's defending counsel told the judge how Drinkwater had worked hard to attain an equal share of the partnership but the terms of his work stipulated that he must be able to drive. If he was disqualified he would have to forfeit his share of the practice and that would cause him tremendous hardship. The judge listened but did not accept the plea. He had already heard how the doctor had two previous convictions in the last two years. He told him:

'I would have taken a lighter view but for the previous convictions. Whatever the calls on you in your practice it is undesirable to have someone driving dangerously around the country.'

The doctor went back to work, to his drinking and drugs, but not to his family. His wife divorced him saying she was 'cruelly offended' by his drinking.

The next step in the doctor's downfall came just a few

months later. Drinkwater was in trouble, looking for a job because the partnership could not have him without his driving licence. He was called in to see an 8-year-old girl, the daughter of an Italian hairdresser called Gerard and his attractive wife, Carole, seventeen years his junior at twenty-seven years old. Gerard had a chain of shops in Reading and the couple lived in an upmarket area. Their daughter, their only child, had tonsilitis and Drinkwater answered Carole's call for someone to come to see the girl and treat her.

The knock on their door that night eventually led to degradation and death in an orgy of sex, pornography, drink and drugs with a camera flashing away at the closing moments of life in a bungalow in the village of Hemsby, a seaside town with the North Sea on one side and the Norfolk Broads on the other.

It was certainly not like that at first. Gerard and Carole were happily married, delighted and rejoicing in their little girl. The doctor changed all that, so much so that later the embittered hairdresser was to accuse him of casting a wicked spell over his wife like a Svengali. But that night the doctor, whom Gerard considered to be a gentleman and like every other doctor he had known, a man of honour and integrity, did his job. He then told the couple how his marriage had broken up and that he was unhappy and Gerard asked him to stay for a drink. Drinkwater stayed and stayed – as he was to on several occasions – drinking gin straight from the bottle and not going home.

Gerard took pity on this handsome man, helping a person he thought was destitute with real troubles. He listened to him, invited him to his house, even drove him round on calls to patients. While this was going on his wife became remote and moody, taking the drugs the doctor prescribed for slimming and migraine.

Her husband had no idea what was going on until one night Drinkwater, who was very drunk, blurted out at the dinner table that Carole was unhappy with him and Carole admitted that this was true when her amazed husband asked her.

Gerard later said that when she left him, taking her

money out of the husband–wife partnership, she was completely under the doctor's influence and suspected that he was dominating her with drugs. Gerard was shattered; Drinkwater and his new love elated. They moved from the royal county of Berkshire to the windswept wilds of the Norfolk coast, and set up home in Hemsby, where the doctor joined the local practice and where Carole became a receptionist at the medical centre.

They became popular in the community, with people knowing they were not married but accepting them as a devoted and happy couple. The doctor kept up a respectable front, meticulous at his work, pleasant and able, hiding his nocturnal activities – that he was a drunkard and drug taker who could turn into a frenzied sex pervert in the night with someone whom he later said was a willing partner.

Carole seemed happy with the man she nicknamed Dr Drink-Gin – because of his habit of pouring drink down his throat straight from a bottle – and ignored her mother's advice that if she stayed with the dashing young doctor she would end up on a mortuary slab. In the evenings they would wander down to the local pub and sit, often holding hands, as he had gin and she Pernod. Then they would buy a bottle of red wine and go home for their meal and lovemaking.

Her husband knew and could not believe what was happening to his wife. She changed from a loving mother to a drinker, a woman who was under the spell of this hard-drinking, drug-taking doctor, as far as he was concerned.

It was not all happiness in the small bungalow. Carole would get upset when her lover rang his ex-wife and talked to her about the children, fearful that he was going to leave her. Later the doctor was to allege that she talked of suicide. But it was not that that ended their affair – it was a fatal sex game.

On Sunday, 2 July 1972, the police were called to the bungalow and there found Carole naked on the bed. What had happened was quite extraordinary. In a sex game of the lewdest kind they had both stripped naked and the doctor – who had bought a Polaroid so that he could take the good pictures he liked to snap – then injected five different drugs into her, four in one combination, all lethal, and then started taking erotic pictures, sometimes of her on her own with different objects, sometimes of the pair of them together, some in black and white, others in colour.

The drugs were to make her relax so that the objects she wanted included in the pictures, such as a wine bottle and a cucumber, would not hurt so much on insertion, the doctor claimed. But whatever he wanted, whatever she desired, it went on and on – as she lay dying on the bed. When he had his pictures he went to sleep, and when he awoke she was dead.

This sobered him up. He was playing Jim Reeves singing 'My Last Affair' when police arrived. Drinkwater made several statements. In the first he said Carole had committed suicide because of marriage problems. He told Detective Chief Superintendent Reg Lester:

'I didn't inject her. She must have done it herself. She has seen me inject patients … Yes, she wanted to end it all. I supplied the means and I feel awful about it … I loved her dearly. I never ceased to love her and I still do.'

He then changed his story. Carole had developed a desire for perverted sex and was a bit kinky, and although he was rather disgusted he went along with it, he claimed. He admitted that he had pumped her with two injections of drugs to help her relax and said: 'I know I was very confused and acting illogically. We had seemed to have sunk so low.'

The post mortem showed that she had died of asphyxia, not by her lover's hand but as a result of the effect of the drugs.

The detectives had a good look round. They found five black and white and one coloured shot of the orgy wrapped in two shirts in the bedroom. There were seven other obscene photographs in the doctor's surgical bag.

He was charged with murder and for the second time stood in the dock at an Assize court, except that the system had been changed so that it was now called a crown court. Before a jury of eleven men and one woman the doctor pleaded not guilty to murdering Carole. He was thirty-seven, she was twenty-eight when she died.

Mr Rodney Bax, QC, outlined the sordid story that he was going to try to prove with the evidence. He alleged that just before her bizarre death it appeared that she was going to leave him because they were no longer happy together. He claimed that the doctor had injected her with the fatal concoction which affected her breathing, a concoction unknown medically and intended to do one thing: stop her breathing. And while she lay there he began to take the pictures. The prosecutor said:

'With that girl dying he took a series of photographs with a Polaroid camera. He put her in extraordinary and lewd positions to satisfy his perverted instincts. In other photographs he appeared with her and experts say that she was not dead at that time.'

Carole was unconscious, and Mr Bax said: 'If he had not filled her with this lethal mixture of drugs, she would not have allowed herself to get into this position. It is the crown's case that this drug mixture was calculated to kill her by asphyxia.' But no one was suggesting that the doctor was involved in holding her. It was a reaction to his lethal cocktail.

The drugs were of the respiratory depressive kind and a forensic scientist said later in the trial that it was the first time in twenty-two years that Pentothal, a general anaesthetic which eventually stopped her breathing, had been referred to his laboratory involving a death. The other drugs were morphine and pethidine. And, said the prosecutor, the unabsorbed drugs in her body would have killed her again.

Drinkwater made three statements, the jury heard, and two of them were lies. In the third, the doctor said:

'She had developed a desire for perverted sex. I was not very willing initially. She wanted me to use such objects as wine bottles. She got partially undressed. It was painful so she asked me to give her something to make it easier. She liked that sort of thing. It was her wish. I was a bit disgusted by it all.'

It was not a view shared by the judge, Mr Justice Thesiger, when he spoke about Carole at the end of the trial.

Before the jury heard Drinkwater's version, from his own mouth in the witness box, they had to look at the pictures, the lewd, extraordinary and disgusting photos, and see a dummy brought into court so that they could see the positions in which Carole lay after being drugged to be photographed.

They heard from the detective chief superintendent in charge of the case, Reg Lester, how Drinkwater told him he bought a camera and said: 'I enjoy photography very much, I am very keen. I try not to take rubbish. I like to take a good picture.' The jury had an exhibition of his art in front of them. Some could hardly bear to look at them.

They also heard from the doctor's counsel, Mr William Howard, QC, before he called his client to give evidence in the modern St Albans courtroom. He told them:

'This is not a case which I anticipate will command your sympathy and I have got to face this probability, but what I do ask is your intelligent understanding and that you approach this case in that state of mind without any prejudice at all.

'It may be that some of the matters brought to your attention may disgust or revolt or shock you but we cannot have any room in this court for those emotions. People do things sometimes which to others of us are odd.

'The real fact in this case is the state of mind of Dr Drinkwater when he gave the injection he undoubtedly did. It is the state of mind of a man who you may think was undoubtedly suffering from the effects of drink or drugs or a combination of both.

'The difficulty arises in this way. There are three possible verdicts – guilty of murder, not guilty of anything, and the third, guilty of manslaughter. It is that verdict to which your attention should be primarily directed.'

And then, on the fourth day of the trial which was attracting national and international attention, the doctor, used to chatting to patients whether civilian or military, an

experienced GP and officer, went into the witness box to
tell twelve more civilians how his 5 foot 5 inch tall
attractive mistress ended up dead in a way that an
ordinary person found difficult to understand. It was up
to the doctor to be in the opposite role to the one he
normally adopted. It was for him to tell what was wrong,
what the details of his behaviour or illness was.

He told how he and Carole had met, how they had
moved in with each other, how he had bought her an
18-carat gold wedding ring. He said: 'She was absolutely
thrilled to have it and wore it all the time.'

Their sexual relationship was normal, although she did
not sleep well and had nightmares because of her
marriage problems and, more so, because of the fact that
her husband had put their daughter in the custody of a
relative in Italy. The doctor said he gave her mild sedatives
to help her sleep.

He said that up to May their sex relationship was 'very
full, very normal and very satisfying'. In June she became
hysterical about telephone calls he made to his former
wife about his children and threatened to leave him. She
became anxious and depressed. It was then that she asked
him to take erotic pictures, sixteen days after he had
bought his instant camera. She did more than ask, the
doctor said, she urged him to do so, while she was naked
and drugged. The doctor gave the jury his reaction to such
a suggestion from his beloved. He said: 'I said it was
rather an unusual sort of thing to do, rather a perverted
thing to do. She was very persistent.'

He gave her Pentothal to put her to sleep and he said
that he had had several doses of amphetamine during the
day. When he started to take the pictures the flash on his
camera did not work.

Next morning Carole drove him to work because he was
still banned and he told her that the pictures had not come
out. During the day he took more pep pills as he saw some
thirty to forty patients, and in the early evening he and
Carole went to the pub. By that time, the doctor said, 'I felt
somewhat euphoric, light-headed and happy-go-lucky.'

Back in the bungalow, over wine and Pernod, Carole

asked him 'to return to the activities of the previous night'.
What did she say, how did she put it, what exactly were
the words she used? asked the judge. He was an
experienced High Court Judge, a former Mayor of
Chelsea; Mr Justice Thesiger was also known as a severe
sentencer and one who made his punishments smart. On
one occasion he made a young journalist who had killed a
pedestrian while driving under the influence of drink,
after being slipped a Mickey Finn on his twenty-first
birthday, sit in court for a week to listen to the daily serial
of similar cases he had to listen to. At the end of the week
the judge gave him four months. On another occasion he
sentenced a mother and daughter who had stolen
woollens from clothes-lines in an Essex seaside town to six
months for some of the thefts to which they had pleaded
guilty. He said he would consider the others and they
would appear in front of him again when they had served
their sentence. They did so and he gave them another six
months – so back into prison they went again.

He also had once told a young pregnant mother that she
should have no more children by her husband to whom
he was about to give eighteen years for manslaughter. He
was one of a breed like Melford Stevenson and Stable who
no longer sit on the benches.

The doctor had his answer to the judge's question. 'She
said she would like me to take erotic-type photographs
with me involved and this would bring us closer together.
She wanted erotic pictures with phallic objects.'

'Did she use the words erotic and phallic?' the judge
asked.

'Yes.'

Drinkwater's counsel, Mr Howard, a very experienced
defender, very smooth, very elegant, making notes with a
gold pencil, asked: 'What was your reaction?'

'I didn't want to do it basically. I said I didn't think it
was a normal decent sort of thing for people to do.'

'And her reaction?' the barrister asked gently.

'She wanted me to do these things and take
photographs so she could look at them for erotic reasons.
She persisted.'

The jury looked at him, studied him. I expect some tried to picture this conversation in the lounge of the small bungalow, the doctor and the hairdresser. Were they sitting? Were they apart or holding hands or cuddling? How were they dressed?

The doctor went on with his answer: 'I gave in to her request because the drugs and alcohol had released my inhibitions, lowered my normal moral standards. I had some fear that if I didn't comply with her requests she would think I didn't love her.'

The jury knew what the requests were. They might, as counsel might have put it, have wondered about a love that needs drugs, alcohol, wine bottles, even cucumbers from the fridge in a seaside bungalow lounge to make it lasting.

So what did Dr Peter Drinkwater, MD, do? Did his love make any suggestions? asked Mr Howard. Yes, she did, indeed she did.

'Yes' said the doctor. 'That I use Pentothal like I had used the night before. She wanted me to start taking pictures with her partly clothed and then some pictures without her clothes with me involved.

'She took her underclothes off, leaving only a dress and slip on. I injected her while she was lying on the settee in the sitting room.'

And when he injected her did he mean to cause her any harm? Mr Howard probed.

'Not at all.' The answer was emphatic.

'Did you intend to kill her?'

'No.'

Mr Howard went on: 'Having injected her what did you do then?'

The doctor said, as if it was the most natural thing in the world: 'I took photographs I felt she wanted.'

Mr Howard said: 'Some of the pictures we have seen showed her naked.'

'I remember taking her clothes off on the settee and carrying her into the bedroom.' He gave her another injection there because he wanted her to stay asleep.

He said that he got a whole Pentothal syringe and

injected it into her during the picture session. Then as she lay unconscious he pushed half a syringe of a sedative tranquillizer mixture into her.

He said: 'I did not contemplate I would be doing her any harm. It did not occur to me that I was putting her in danger.' But he had already told the jury that his inhibition had gone.

'I didn't think I would be endangering her life' he declared. 'I didn't think any harm would come to her. I loved her dearly. I never once ceased to love her and I still do.'

And then he went to bed, he told the jury, late on Friday afternoon. The trial was adjourned for the weekend. Drinkwater went back to the remand prison; Carole's husband stayed at home; their daughter remained with relatives in Italy. The jury had to wait until Monday morning, the fifth day of the trial, to hear what happened next in this incredible story.

Dr Drinkwater was first woken at 7 a.m. by a phone call which he answered. He then went back to the bed he was sharing with the woman he loved. What did he notice about her? asked Mr Howard.

'She was, as far as I was concerned, asleep tucked down under the sheets. I didn't consider there was anything wrong with her. I didn't even think there was anything wrong with her.'

He was then disturbed by two more calls so he went into the kitchen to make a cup of tea. He looked in the sink.

He said quietly, recalling the terrible moment: 'In the sink I saw the syringes and two open packets of the drug Pentothal. I then recalled the events of the previous night.'

It was a similar situation to that which occurred eleven years earlier to another killer, United States Air Force sergeant Willis Boshears. He dreamed that he strangled a girl he had invited home for New Year's Eve in his sleep and woke to find her dead in bed. Like Drinkwater he panicked. The jury believed him and he walked free.

The doctor went on: 'I was absolutely panic stricken about how Carole would be. I rushed into the bedroom and pulled the bedclothes back. She was lying with her face on the left side. I noticed that her face was swollen and there was a mark on her upper lip. I thought in horror, I didn't or couldn't believe she was dead. I felt her pulse and waited but I couldn't feel one.'

The doctor's voice wavered as he continued: 'I felt her heart but I couldn't feel anything. I gave her extra cardiac stimulation. I did this for a few minutes but there was no heart response. All the time I was saying "Oh God no, please don't be dead, I love you darling" and things like that.'

He tried more desperate measures. He filled a syringe with a respiratory drug and tried to inject it into her veins and arms. But he failed. The needle would not go in. He took one more attempt to revive her: he plunged the needle directly into her heart. There was no reaction. The doctor said: 'When this failed I knew she was dead. I sat on the side of the bed and wept, I sobbed. I loved her so much.'

And as he wept Jim Reeves sang. The doctor put on Reeves' record of 'My Last Affair'. It was, he explained, for sentimental reasons. 'I liked it and she liked it. It was rather a sad song,' he said.

Then he pulled himself together. He tidied up the house and shaved. He put his love back into position in the bed and called another doctor. In his panic and confusion he decided to make up a story that Carole had committed suicide.

He explained: 'I thought she must have suffocated to death. I wanted to cover up the perverted sex acts of the previous night for Carole's sake so I decided to make up the story that she had committed suicide.'

Mr Howard came back to the injection. 'Did you think the injection you gave her would be fatal?'

The doctor shook his head, 'No I didn't intend it to be' he said.

Then he was cross-examined by the prosecutor, Mr Bax. He asked how Carole got the injuries to her face. The doctor thought she must have received them when he put her upside down on the floor with her face on the floor to take one of the photographs. He denied that he had injected the woman he loved with a fatal dose. 'It was not a fatal dose' he insisted.

'What then do you think killed her?' Mr Bax asked.

Drinkwater answered: 'I thought she had suffocated, face down on the bed having been heavily sedated and unable to correct her position in order that she could breathe.'

The prosecutor put it to him straight and direct. 'I am suggesting that you are not telling the truth. The administration of the drug was a deliberate act.'

Not so, the doctor answered. 'I was not trying to harm her.'

Mr Bax gave his view of that answer and everything else the doctor had said, in his closing speech to the jury. He chose his words carefully and said:

'There were only two people in that bungalow that night. One is dead and the other is a man who you may think will lie and change his lies and then lie again to suit the purpose at any given time.

'You may think that the man by his attitude to drugs either in relationship to himself or to the woman he professed to love, proved himself to be wholly irresponsible and a very dangerous man.

'A very dangerous man ... grossly negligent,' said Mr Bax.

He went on, for he was not finished by any means. 'The first story the defendant put up to mislead the police was that the dead woman had committed suicide. Why did he put that story? There is only one answer.

'He knew that there had been a killing and he knew that he had done the killing otherwise he need only have said: "I gave her a sedative mixture to put her into a nice long sleep and she must have suffocated in the bedclothing. It was an accident." Why didn't he say that?

'The reason he said she committed suicide was that he knew and still does know what he had given her. It is consistent with the dark and guilty secret that he had given her a fatal dose.

'If those obscene photographs had not emerged this

case would have been written off as suicide and the course of justice would have been averted.'

He put it simply: 'He is a doctor, a professional man and a self-confessed liar.'

The doctor's counsel had the help of a professional witness, a Harley Street consultant, who said Drinkwater's story was consistent with his claim that he was intoxicated with drugs and drink and in a 'devil may care' mood the night Carole died. Mr Howard told the jury in his closing speech to them:

'So many wives had said to their husbands "I wish I was dead" but it doesn't mean a thing. We know that Carole left her husband for Dr Drinkwater. I ask you not to sit in judgement of that. Carole was deeply attracted to the doctor.'

He showed the jury a different photograph to the filthy ones they had seen before. This time the doctor and his love were clothed and together like a normal couple. Mr Howard commented: 'These pictures tell a story all their own of a couple who are happy together with one another. Do you think it was plausible that he was plotting her death?

'If a doctor plans murder he has many ways at his command of executing it and he does not do it in the state that he was in. The offence is not to be excused because he took drink and drugs.

'The right verdict is one of manslaughter.'

That was the verdict they returned by a ten to two majority. If a jury cannot come to a unanimous conclusion the judge can direct them that they can consider a majority where ten of their number are agreed. In this case they decided it was not murder but manslaughter by a majority verdict.

The judge had made up his mind about the dashing doctor and his stories. He did not believe a word of them. He told him what he thought about his claim that it was Carole's idea that he should take erotic pictures of her. Said Mr Justice Thesiger from his throne:

'Reports show her to have been a charming and lovable girl. I don't believe for one moment that she could have suggested these practices and invited him to put her under that they could take place.'

Drinkwater, he said, was an intelligent but a dangerous man.

'It is impossible' he said 'to imagine more reckless conduct for a man who had had two warnings about consuming drugs.'

But he had made one mistake. He left the pictures in his bag, his surgical bag, among the instruments and pills for curing the sick. 'That was his only mistake' the judge said 'leaving those pictures to be discovered.'

That mistake, which gave detectives the lead they needed to prove it was not the suicide that Drinkwater claimed, cost him dear. It cost him his Carole whom he planned to marry as soon as she was free; it cost him his job because he did not oppose the application to have him struck off; it cost him his name and his liberty.

The judge jailed him for twelve years. As Drinkwater was taken away from St Albans to a London prison to await a placing in another jail to serve his long sentence, Carole's husband accused him in words that had to be bottled up until after the trial because only facts and not comment can be reported until that time. The hatred, the venom, the loathing, the despair and the misery of what he had lost when the doctor took his lovely wife off and then killed her, leaving him a widower and his only child an orphan, spewed out to the press who came to ask his opinion of the verdict and what had happened to the wife he loved.

In his home the Italian-born hairdresser said with hatred in his heart that Drinkwater was a scoundrel who had bewitched his wife and turned her into a drug-crazy wreck and then a corpse. It was because she helped him with his problems, of which he had plenty. And before she ran off eleven months before she died she was like a woman in a dream and her husband could not get through to her. She seemed remote and the only person who had any effect on her was the doctor.

In the end the doctor tried to save his skin by branding Carole as a pervert, her husband said. But people would remember her as she really was, a lovely girl without an evil thought in her body.

He summed up his loneliness, his distraught state in this way: 'That man destroyed our whole life and then he destroyed my wife. We were very happy. I loved her more than anything else in the whole world.'

He was not the only one who was angry and desperately unhappy over what had happened. Carole's mother had also despaired over Drinkwater. As well as warning her daughter that she would end up on a mortuary slab if she stayed with him, she had tried to stop such a situation happening. She had noticed the bad bits of the doctor's bizarre behaviour: the way he demanded 'barmaid get the bar open' when he arrived and poured gin down his throat from the bottle; how he worked himself into a frenzy as he played a set of drums that Carole's husband had bought for their little girl, finally smashing the set to pieces; how he domineered Carole, who changed into a gin-drinking, heavy-smoking woman, almost a zombie. She was strongly against him but it made no difference: Carole was not going to listen to her down-to-earth Yorkshire mother.

The doctor's former wife also talked about her feelings. She just could not believe what the man to whom she had been married for twelve years had done.

She said: 'It was like hearing about a complete stranger. The evidence shocked me. He was never like that when we were married.'

Their sex life was normal and fine and the only trouble was his drinking, which became so bad that it led to divorce. It was after they had split up that he met Carole and his former wife allowed the children to go to stay with them.

From his prison cell Drinkwater kept in touch. He wrote to her to say that the 'whole thing was a tragic accident'.

After the trial was over and the doctor was seven months into his sentence, his leave to appeal against it was heard in the Appeal Court. The judges were completely unsympathetic. They heard a plea from the doctor's counsel that the sentence was crushing and that it would cause hardship to his ex-wife and children whom he was supporting. But Mr Justice Roskill, turning down the application for leave to appeal, said that they could not be swayed in this case by considerations of mercy, for the sentence was abundantly justified. 'It was,' said the judge, 'horrifying – as near murder as one can possibly get.'

A week later an application was made to the General Medical Council disciplinary committee that he be struck off the medical register. Dr Peter Drinkwater was not there and did not offer any defence. The committee heard the briefest of detail as to what he had done and what had happened to him and struck him off.

Plain Mr Peter Drinkwater stayed in jail, did his sentence, came out and started a new life.

He used the phrase 'tragic accident' when he wrote to his ex-wife. The jury had decided that it was no accident. But it was tragic. He was a man who started life with everything, followed a path that led only to a good life in sport and medicine, and threw it all away because of his unquenchable thirst for drink and drugs which turned him into everything a doctor should not be. It was not as though he was not warned. Twice officialdom rightly stepped in and told him to behave himself. But the self-destruct button had been pressed and he did not turn back as he could so easily have done. Instead he blew his life up.

11

Hopkins

Child Abductor and Pervert

The end of the 1985 summer season was almost in sight as the battered brown Rover turned out of the vast caravan village at Great Yarmouth on the Norfolk coast to head for the west. The rain beat down on the 15,000 caravans that covered the enormous site and on the club where holidaymakers enjoyed a drink and a disco. For some it was the last night of their holiday before heading home and a long autumn and winter of work. For one pair, a mother and a daughter, it was a night to celebrate before going back to a refuge for battered wives in north London. They were making the most of it.

The driver of the Rover had been described by some as a fat man, but that was three years earlier when the police had been looking for him. He had slimmed down now and was a little sad to be leaving Yarmouth because he was greatly attracted to the place. He had had a successful visit three months earlier, on the same caravan park, just before the holidaymakers arrived in their thousands to enjoy life on the bracing east coast, with the sun and the sand that stretched in its golden beauty for miles. But the driver's sadness at leaving was definitely outweighed by the anticipation of what was to come.

On the back seat of his car was a little girl, blue-eyed, blonde, with her hair down to her shoulders, just three years old. She had been woken when the man came into the caravan, letting himself in with a key. Of course he should not have been in the caravan because it was not the one in which he was staying. Nor should the little girl have been alone; but her mother had arranged a baby sitter who did not turn up. Expecting her to do so at any moment, the little girl's mother took a chance and went with friends to the club, leaving the little girl tucked up and asleep in bed. But this stranger had woken her and carried her to his car and put her on the back seat, and she had gone back to sleep again.

As the rain drove down in the lazy wind that sweeps across East Anglia from the Urals, only to be broken by the Gog Magog Hills 80 miles to the west just past Cambridge, the car headed towards Norwich 20 miles away. It was a dead straight road for about 8 miles past the banks of the Broads where boats were moored and the occupants slept. There was little traffic about, but what there was could be spotted from a long way off, the headlights just pinpoints in the night, gradually becoming brighter and larger as they approached, and then only the dark again.

Through the bends at Acle the car went and the little girl slept on. The driver had two thoughts on his mind: to carry on driving without the police stopping him on a routine check, for then he would have to tell them a story to explain why the girl was on the back seat (perhaps he was the father, although that might be difficult if the girl woke and started screaming), but much more important was what he was going to do with her.

He went through Norwich, using the ring road, until he reached the A11, the main road to London. It is a single-lane road for most of the way but it is straight and fast, particularly when there is no traffic at all on it. He put his foot down and the Rover's powerful engine responded. He headed first for Wymondham and its by-pass and then on to Attleborough and that town's new bypass. The new bypasses have cut minutes off the journey west. From Attleborough the road becomes even straighter and faster, and when it goes past the Snetterton motor racing circuit it is very straight for miles through the Stanford Battleground where the Army train. The rain was still coming down and the little girl slept and the man savoured what was to come.

There was no search for his car, the Rover with false number plates (for he had changed them before taking the little girl from her bed.) No one had yet noticed that the little girl had gone. The disco was still in full blast in the club and the rain was beating down on the caravans, and the one in which the little girl had slept so happily and soundly was empty.

He skirted Thetford and was on the stretch down to Elveden and past the war memorial which towers above the forest at that point and then sweeping down towards Barton Mills and his destination. He knew just where he was going. On an undeveloped film in his camera were shots of a man-made canal near a picnic site not far from Barton Mills over the border into Suffolk. He knew what he was doing when he took those pictures on a reconnaissance early that summer. The canal was a relief for the River Lark and the spot he had picked was not far from the vast American Air Force base at Royal Air Force Mildenhall. The base is the gateway to Europe for tens of thousands of American Air Force personnel. The canal was an ideal hiding place, one of millions, as we know, in Norfolk.

When he stopped the little girl woke. It was dark and she was on the back seat of a car; she did not know where she was, she did not know where her mummy was, she was frightened and she started to scream. She had very good reason to scream: she was in mortal danger.

The driver of the car turned to her with overpowering perverted lust in his heart. It consumed and totally engulfed him.

Three years before, on the same date, 13 September, the driver had taken another little girl from a caravan on a seaside site while her mother was out having a drink. But this girl, a blonde too, was ten years old, old enough to remember the man and what had happened in great detail and give police a description which was to come in very useful in 1985 when the younger child was taken from her bed.

The 10-year-old in her pyjamas answered the knock at the caravan door on the site at St Osyth near Clacton in Essex, another very popular holiday area. The man appeared perfectly normal, and why not? Sex perverts and molesters look no different to anyone else. The difference is in the way they act when they are with their victims, when the urge that is within them bursts out like a dam wall breaking and no power on earth can stop it.

The man, in his early thirties perhaps, smart and about 5 foot 6 or 7 inches tall, a bit chubby, told the girl called Pauline that he was a minicab driver and asked if she had a silver necklace with the letter P on it. She said she had and he said that was all right because her mother had asked him to come and collect her. She had no hesitation in going with him because he seemed so genuine.

But once inside the car, a dark-coloured Rover, he changed totally. He tied her up and gagged her. The girl began to cry and thought about the boy at her school who had been murdered and was certain that that was going to be her fate.

The man drove from the site and headed east. It was to be a 90-mile journey east back to his favourite place, Great Yarmouth. The girl was crying through her gag and eventually her captor, who had string in his car to tie her, just as he carried orange string when he was driving the 3-year-old through the night, took the gag out and talked to her.

Her conversation saved her life. She managed to keep calm and told him about her mother and their love of animals and how her mother was a member of an anti-vivisection group. The man told her that he was an animal lover too, they had a bond in common. He said that once he had broken into a vivisection centre. He did not tell her that among his criminal activities for which he had gone to prison was burglary.

They went on talking through the long drive, through the hours of the night, into the early hours as finally they arrived in Great Yarmouth. The man had talked but he had not touched her. Their mutual love of animals had turned him off.

He dumped her in a toilet block in the town and drove off. She stood there tied in women's underwear from another caravan and then went to find a policeman.

The girl said later that she was sure she was not killed because they had something in common. The courageous girl lived to tell the police and her mother, and when, three years later, it was discovered that the 3-year-old was not in her bed and a major search for her started, Pauline's mother rang the police and reminded them of the man her daughter described as chubby or fat.

She was not the only girl to meet up with him. Three months before the 3-year-old girl disappeared he was in Yarmouth as usual and this time he was peering through a caravan window as a 14-year-old girl undressed. The man became excited and broke into the caravan and grabbed the girl after tying her up with a bra. But she was bigger and stronger than his 10-year-old victim and she fought. He threatened her with a 9-inch knife, for he was a man who always carried a knife to show how big he was. The knife did not frighten the girl enough as she screamed for help just before eleven at night. She kept on struggling, and as she did so he plunged the blade into her back, creating a wound which later needed four stitches. It did not stop her. She ran for her life and escaped. The man, who had been a caller at a stall on Yarmouth seafront in the past, and knew the town and the camps extremely well, drove off into the night.

Police searched for him but it was difficult in a holiday town packed with thousands whose only interest was enjoyment and where many single men and women were looking for partners to have a good time together at the funfair, on the beach, in the restaurants, the cafés, the bars and the discos.

Three months later, on Friday September 13, the man was back again at the caravan park and struck lucky again, because little Leoni Williams (not her real name) was on her own and sound asleep in the caravan. She was only three but she had led a varied life. She did not have much of promise in her life except for love from her mother Gail and her estranged father David who had tried (but failed) shortly before that date to get a custody order.

Leoni had lived in a number of London lodgings and hippy communes and for the past eight months in a women's aid centre for battered wives in London. It was part of the scheme at this hostel that they had a break away from London and that was why they were having a week's holiday in the caravan at the seaside.

On the last night of the holiday Gail had arranged for a babysitter for Leoni, who had had supper at 8.15 p.m. and gone to bed and straight to sleep because she had had a marvellous day playing out in the fresh air and on the beach. Gail was going to the club with Leoni's half-sister, aged thirteen, and two older children staying in the caravan. By 9.30 p.m. Leoni had fallen sound asleep, and half an hour later, when the baby sitter was due but had not arrived, Gail decided to chance it because the girl was so deeply asleep. She locked the door of the caravan and the small group went off.

Half an hour later, at 10.30 p.m., a man let himself into caravan K50 and took the little girl. A few minutes later the baby sitter arrived, discovered the caravan empty and presumed that Gail had decided to take Leoni with her, and left. By that time Leoni was on her way to Barton Mills.

When she woke up she screamed. The man was ready for that. He put his hand over her mouth while he tied her with the orange string he had bought on the camp, the same string that was used by holidaymakers to hang curtains and washing. Then he finished his journey to the picnic place he had found earlier in the year, the place he had photographed. The little girl was just minutes from the end of her short life. He sexually assaulted her, the only reason for the kidnap, and then he picked her up.

A little later Leoni's mother arrived back at the caravan to find that her daughter was missing. She and her other daughter and friends began searching because the little girl had disappeared twice before during the holiday. She was a strong-willed, active child who liked her own way and had no fear.

The search could not find her and next day it became a

national event. A little child missing on a seaside holiday camp is always national news, particularly if the child is only three and blue-eyed with blonde hair.

The police arrived in force and campers joined in. Many were going home but they all searched round their caravans before they went. Those staying and those arriving helped. Every possible place was checked as far away as the sea, because the police knew that a child of that age could walk a long way, certainly more than a mile or two if really determined.

There was no sign of her. The disappearance reunited her mother and her father, who had arrived to help. They stayed together at the camp, waiting for news.

The police made out a timetable of everything they knew. Gail had left Leoni sleeping at 10.00 p.m. The baby sitter arrived at 10.47 p.m. and, finding the caravan open and empty, presumed Leoni was with her mother, and left.

At 11.05 p.m. the family staying in a nearby caravan heard a child crying 'Mummy, mummy' but did nothing. On a site that large, children are always crying. It was a familiar sound. The same sort of call from a child was heard by another family in another caravan in the area an hour later, and then nearly two hours later at 1.45 a.m. on the Sunday morning. None of them reported the cries. There really was no reason for them to do so.

But by that time Leoni was over 70 miles away near the picnic site 150 yards from the main roundabout at Barton Mills on the A1065 road.

The days ticked by, each minute like an hour for her desperate parents. Her mother blamed herself for leaving the child. It was only natural, but it did not help the hunt. That went on relentlessly, policemen as eager to find the child as anyone else. Most were family men.

There was nothing, just vague spottings of strange men, old vehicles, all noted. The little girl – and in the county of Norfolk it was almost a cliché – had vanished without trace: one moment she was tucked up in bed, the next she was gone.

To policemen who had lived through April and Steven

and Pamela and Susan Long and the body at Cockley Cley and Heidi Reddin it had that eerie pattern.

It was luck that solved the mystery of what had happened and it came four days later. The man, the once chubby man, who had taken the little girl from her bed, had found one of Norfolk's hiding places, but what he had not bargained for was the fact that the weeds and the man-made sluices would stop a body being eventually washed out to sea. The body of Leoni was found floating face down, her hands tied behind her back, her pyjama trousers missing, in the release channel just into Suffolk. When she was spotted by a woman taking her dog for a walk she thought she was looking at a broken toy.

The police took the body from the silt, told the heart-broken parents, and started looking for the man who had done it. They started checking on everyone who had a conviction for sex offences and tried to link them with Great Yarmouth.

They had this vague description of a man with a battered car, possibly a Rover type, but many men have battered cars. What they did have was the description by 10-year-old Pauline of the man who snatched her three years earlier at St Osyth in Essex and drove and dumped her at Great Yarmouth. And there was the 14-year-old girl who had been grabbed from her caravan three months earlier on the same site; her description of her attacker matched that of Pauline.

They were looking, they rightly thought, for a man in his late twenties or early thirties, about 5 foot 6 or 7 inches tall, chubby, with a moustache and a love for Yarmouth and a perverted lust for little girls.

Criminal Records provided the list to follow, the catalogue of possible suspects out of whom might come the killer, a man who had committed a crime described by Chief Detective Superintendent Eric Shields as 'callous and horrific'. It was a low-key description because any man who can take a little girl from her bed, tie and rape her and then throw her into a ditch in the middle of the night has a mind that no normal person can understand.

But who was this man? One of the names turned up by

the Record Office computer was Gary Hopkins, aged twenty-eight, jobless, a thief with convictions for burglary, assault on police and indecent exposure. He was also known to have been in Yarmouth.

As a matter of routine he was visited by the police, along with many others. On such occasions the task of going to see someone, usually just for elimination (because, unlike in fiction, it is a long tedious but essential job), is left to the force in whose area the person lives. In Bedford the job was given to Detective Constable Paul Wright. He was thirty and had just been promoted from the traffic department and was keen to win his laurels and show that he was going to be a good detective.

He was sent round to Hopkins' home on the normal routine 'trace, interview and eliminate' check which Suffolk had asked for (they being the force looking for the killer because, although Leoni had been abducted in Great Yarmouth in Norfolk, the body was found just over the border into Suffolk). When he met Hopkins face to face, the new detective was not happy. Hopkins had an alibi and gave it. But Wright, who had a young daughter, was not at all sure that the man sitting opposite him was telling the truth. There was something about him, something that gave him a gut feeling that Hopkins was lying, that he could in fact be the little girl's killer, a man who could have thrown her into the water.

He probed and probed and it became clear to him that Hopkins fitted the vague reports the police in Great Yarmouth had had of a man seen around the caravan site about the time that Leoni vanished.

Hopkins was calm and confident, but the detective was to say later that there was something about him that did not 'gel'. For instance: he had shaved off his moustache in the winter, an odd thing to do. He kept questioning. Hopkins said that he had not been at the caravan site during the time the little girl was there. Then he said he had been there a week earlier, and his girl friend said he was a regular visitor, when he was vague. When he was asked about his car he was also evasive and said he had not got one.

The questioning, chat-style almost because he was not a suspect, just a man to be eliminated, went on and Hopkins said well yes, he had had an old Rover but he had sold it. 'Who to?' the new detective constable asked, and no doubt his adrenalin was flowing because he was certain that he was on to something. He made Hopkins go and get the receipt from the garage to whom he had sold it, and then went round there to make more inquiries.

The police in East Anglia had information about a brown Rover with a sticker in the rear window being seen on the site, along, of course, with many other cars. The car that Hopkins had sold was an old brown Rover with a sticker in the back. The description of the man, the car, fitted the sketchy information that was given by witnesses on the site. DC Wright went back to tell his superiors; they rang Suffolk, who came roaring down the road to Bedford.

Fifty-six days after Leoni was taken from her bed and caravan her killer was arrested and driven back down the road he had taken after dumping her in the water. By that time Hopkins had been fingerprinted and photographed and his prints matched those found after the earlier abduction on the site. The artist's impression that the detective saw was a match of the man he had interviewed, Gary Hopkins.

His trial began on 23 June 1986 at Ipswich crown court. It was a modern, airy court and Hopkins, smartly dressed, had a spacious dock to share with two prison officers. He pleaded not guilty to murdering Leoni but guilty to kidnapping her.

The jury of eight men and four women were sworn in and the prosecutor, Mr Michael Hill, QC, quietly outlined the grotesque story of which nightmares are made. It was a distressing, terrible account of the last hours of the little girl's life. He told it factually, going from moment to moment, laying it out without passion or emotion so that the jury understood exactly what had happened, but leaving to their imagination the full horror of it all.

He told them how Hopkins had a series of tearful interviews with the police in which he described how he travelled from home in Bedford to the caravan site at Great

Yarmouth where he prowled around armed with a bunch of skeleton keys. He used one of those keys to enter the caravan where the little girl was sound asleep. According to Hopkins she suddenly appeared while he was rifling a suitcase and it was that moment which sealed her fate.

He said that he remembered nothing until he found himself driving towards Norwich with Leoni in the back of his car. He was on the A11, heading towards Newmarket, Cambridge and London when she woke and began screaming. He said he pulled into a gateway and dragged the struggling little girl from the car, clapping his hand over her mouth, and then carried her into a pine wood at the Barton Mills picnic site where he admitted sexually assaulting her.

And what happened then? There were two versions. Hopkins told the police that after satisfying his perverted lust he left the 3-year-old girl trussed up but alive in the pitch black in the wood. But the prosecution claimed that he tossed her into the water, her hands tied together, alive. For, to add horror on horror, the little girl died from drowning.

To disprove Hopkins' story that the little girl fell into the water the prosecutor said that she could never have made her way through the pine trees, the undergrowth and brambles and scrambled down the steep 15-foot bank into the water without scratching her bare legs because, as you will recall, Hopkins had removed her blue pyjama trousers. Yet there were no scratch marks on her little legs. Even to suggest that someone else had put her in to drown was fantastic and incredible.

No, said the prosecutor: 'The crown says this man took that child there and killed her by throwing her or putting her bodily into that water.'

Hopkins claimed he did not know that the man-made drainage channel ran through the wood, the jury was told, but five months before the kidnap he had taken eight photographs of the site and they were found on an unprocessed film at his home.

Hopkins cried when a police inspector told how the body was found. He continued to cry as a constable gave more details. When the jury were shown the pictures he had taken of the murder scene he collapsed in the dock and had to be taken to the cells for twenty minutes to recover.

Then they heard how Hopkins offered to show police where he had assaulted Leoni. Police Constable Malcom Lumden said that Hopkins' mood changed as they approached the site, becoming fidgety and moving about in his seat. He went on: 'You could feel an aura about him. As we approached the picnic spot he became visibly white. The blood drained from his face and he started breathing heavily and yawning. He started looking straight ahead. He said something about a sports car on a garage forecourt, then we came to the picnic area he became quiet again. He said no more until we arrived at the police station.'

When the prosecution case ended, the defence counsel, Mr Brian Cox, QC, said that Hopkins would not be giving evidence.

In his closing speech, the prosecutor said:

'He carted that child off and, having satisfied his perverted lust, he disposed of her in the hope that none of these events would be traced to him.

'It is the crown's case that the evidence demonstrates that he put her in the water and he did it because he wanted her to drown so that he would not be at risk.

'That's murder.'

He went on: 'How did that child get into the water if he did not put her there? Imagine that child in the dark with her hands bound behind her and ask yourself in all common sense how did she get out of the wood where he left her and into the water without a mark on her.'

The jury never heard what Hopkins had to say from his own lips. But they did hear what he told the police:

'After what I had done I expected a good hiding and I deserved it. I remember being in the caravan and the little girl coming out. The next thing I remember is driving out and then I remember her screaming in the woods.'

They found him guilty, and once that had happened their duty was over; but they stayed to the end for the judge had to hear the details about the other two girls, the one aged ten at St Osyth in 1982 and the 14-year-old a few months before Leoni was murdered. Hopkins admitted abduction, burglary of women's clothing including underwear, and wounding the 14-year-old at Yarmouth.

Then a senior detective gave the details of Hopkins' previous convictions. They went back to 1974, and in the last nine years he had been sentenced to more than three years in prison for indecent exposure, assault on police and burglary.

He had once been a student nurse but had money problems and marriage problems and at the time of the murder was living with his common law wife.

The judge did not waste or mince words on him. The sentence was mandatory, for murder automatically carries life. But a judge can recommend the minimum that the killer serves. Mr Justice Mann told Hopkins: 'The circumstances of Leoni's death display a degree of callousness and depravity which is almost unbelievable. It is quite clear from reports that you are a menace to the public and that there is no prospect of that menace disappearing. For the indefinite future you will pose a threat to young girls.' He sentenced him to four life terms for the murder and kidnapping of Leoni and the kidnapping of the other two girls, and recommended that he should serve not less than twenty-five years, a quarter of a century.

No one had any doubt that that was what he deserved. Just to imagine quickly what he did brings revulsion flowing up like a fountain of disgust.

What was interesting after the end of the trial and the sentence, as he was taken away, was the reaction of those involved.

There was the little girl's mother. She was distraught with guilt when Leoni first went missing and it was understandable. She wept often during the trial and afterwards talked of her feelings now it was over. She did not blame herself any more although she still felt guilty and mourned her daughter. Any mother would have done the same. But to manage to go on after such an appalling disaster she rationalized it, saying that it was not her who killed her, it was not her responsibility. She said, and she was right, that there were hundreds of other children left alone that night on the camp site, and all those mothers, when Leoni was abducted, must have said to themselves that it could have been their child who was taken.

The little girl's father was more down to earth in what he had to say. He said, with considerable justification, that Hopkins' life in jail was going to be terrible. As a child killer of the worst and depraved kind he would suffer and go on suffering as he rotted in a cell, his torment going on and on and on.

Then there was Hopkins' family. They told of his background, his life, the backcloth to a man who could take a little girl from her bed, tie her hands behind her back, assault her in the most foul sexual manner and then toss her like a rag doll into the water in pitch black and walk away and go home to his common law wife. What manner of man was he?

The truth was, as so often, that he was nothing much at all. He was a nobody who had in his mind desires so bizarre and beyond the range of normal minds that no one could guess this evil lust was there and could erupt in such a way.

He was born in Romford and was never sure of who his father was. He was sexually assaulted several times when he was six, was taken into care and drifted into jobs and petty crime.

He met his first common law wife in 1975 and they have a son. A daughter died – a cot death victim. He was quizzed about that, and when it was suggested he had mistreated the baby he ran into a park and indecently exposed himself. It was possibly the reaction of a distraught father. No one thought he might do the things he did later.

He met his wife while he was working as a nursing auxiliary at the hospital in Romford where he was born. They had a daughter, but the marriage was wrecked by rows and the fact that his wife found him dressed in her clothes.

Then he met Janet, with whom he lived with her two children in Bedford. They were bingo mad. They met as her marriage was ending at Great Yarmouth. She was staying on the camp where Hopkins snatched Leoni. He was a bingo stall caller, but also a thief, and he went to jail for stealing from the stall.

She waited and when he was released they set up home and she said that their sex life was quite normal and healthy. After the trial she said she just could not believe that same man had done those terrible things to a little girl. She thought Hopkins, who boasted quite untruthfully that he had been in the SAS, was off doing burglaries when he disappeared. She had no reason to suspect him. Why should she?

How many men secrete their real desires, lusts, yearnings in a separate part of their mind is something that does not appear in annual statistics. Any attempt to give figures is guesswork because unless a man or woman is confessing on a psychiatrist's couch, how is anyone to know? Everyone knows that Sonia Sutcliffe had no idea that her husband was the Yorkshire Ripper, and there are a few cases similar to that. The M5 rapist and the Cambridge rapist carried on perfectly normal lives in between crazed attacks on women; in the Cambridge rapist's case it was so bad that in the end he wore a black leather mask with slits for eyes and mouth and the word 'rapist' in paint over the forehead.

Some men can cover their most evil thoughts and doings while intoxicated almost to the point of unconsciousness with alcohol. Kim Philby was a good example. Even when practically incoherent with drink he still did not drop one hint that he was a Russian spy. His partners, Maclean and Burgess, were equally adept at covering what they were up to even when tongues were loosened far past the danger point of other men. But what is the danger point? Who is to say that the nice man in the smart suit with the glass in his hand, speaking quietly and politely to a woman, is not a raging beast who has lusts that are unspeakable and, if put into practice, disgust and revolt? It is not something that is money- or class-related.

Public schoolboys may yearn to continue their upbringing by being smacked by phantasy nannies or caned by substitute figures of their prefects or masters, but that is not serious. Ordinary secondary school educated children may grow into adults with unbearable and wicked desires too. It goes deeper than that. I remember in a Yorkshire pit village a burly miner who could not keep his hands off the pigs or his wife. He would go from one to another after a few drinks in the miners' welfare, and died in the sty with a boar on a dark night. Where did that amazing desire come from that was hidden from public and marital view?

So Hopkins followed a pattern of invisible evil. He also, although Janet did not know, managed to find another woman, Jackie, while all this was going on. They were just friends, but while he was in prison on remand awaiting trial he wrote to her after she had written saying she wanted to marry him if Janet did not, and, like Janet, she was ready to wait for him. He had already slipped an engagement ring on Janet's finger in jail.

She, like Janet, found him a warm, caring man with a sense of humour. A child lover too. There was nothing in his make-up and behaviour to suggest that he was anything other. Jackie, whose own father was murdered by a crazed relative, accepted Hopkins' explanation that Leoni's death was an accident and that he panicked.

Janet, the woman with whom he lived, just could not believe it all. He wrote countless letters to her and said that he did not know why it happened and that he could never excuse himself, although he never gave any explanation.

Now he is serving his sentence in solitary confinement because he knows that if he ever chooses to mix with the other prisoners he will be given terrible punishment. Even the worst robbers cannot stand men who do bad things to children. They are fathers themselves. To add to the legal punishment he has been given is one of his own making, because the man who liked to prowl in the night after girls suffers from claustrophobia, and being locked up on his own will be almost unbearable.

Many, if not all, will say that as he cannot be hanged that is just.

12

Pole

Christmas Rapist and Killer

On the long stretch of road through Swaffham Forest on Monday 28 December 1986 two cars were travelling in the opposite direction. It was a crisp morning and the Christmas holidays were in full swing. There were not many cars on the A1065 at that time but the two that were there were there for entirely different reasons.

In one were the Smiths (not their real name) on a day's outing to see relatives. The parents, Derek and Diane, had been married for two years and in the car with them was Diane's 5-year-old son Terry by her first marriage, and in the carry cot on the back seat was 5-month-old Gemma. They were as happy as any young family on a day out could be: laughing, chatting, content with life.

Coming the other way, totally unknown to them, was a homicidal maniac called Peter Chmilowskyj, known as Pete the Pole, whose sole interest at that moment was to crash the dark-blue hired car he was driving way above the speed limit into an oncoming vehicle, preferably a lorry, to kill himself.

A terrified 17-year-old girl crouched beside him. She had already written a suicide note to her parents, saying goodbye and asking the plaintive, terrifying, mind-numbing question: 'Why did it have to be me?' Why indeed? She had been kidnapped by the man beside her, a massive 16 stone, 6 foot 3 inch body-building fanatic whose whole adult life was built around rape and assault, all in revenge, he claimed, for the way he had been treated as a child by his mother. He grabbed the pretty girl called Samantha, who shook with fear beside him, after another kidnap and rape orgy just a few days before Christmas. That girl had escaped after being raped ten times over three days and Samantha replaced her, tricked into the car just after midnight on Christmas Day, thinking it was a minicab to take her home.

Now she faced death because Pete the Pole, son of a Ukrainian father and German mother, wanted to die in sorrow for what he had done, but also blaming the beatings and the terrible treatment he had received as a child and being put in homes.

Pete the Pole was driving at 70 to 80 m.p.h. as he approached the village of Hilborough, ready for death. He had tried this once before when in trouble some years before, but the oncoming vehicle had swerved out of the way. This time there were going to be no mistakes.

The two cars closed in on each other. Derek Smith had no inkling about what was going to happen. One moment he was driving along on his own side of the road, noticing a dark blue car coming on the other side at a very fast speed. Then, without warning, no hoot on the horn, no flashing lights, no warning that death was about to come in the quiet of a Norfolk morning, the dark car swung across the road and smashed straight into the Smiths' car. There was silence after that appalling sound that comes from crunching metal and smashing glass as it collides at over 100 miles an hour.

Pete the Pole was still alive. So was his victim, weeping and screaming beside him after that initial eerie silence. So too were the Smiths, Derek and Diane and her son. Baby Gemma was the only one to die at the hands of a wicked man who sought death.

The Smiths were injured, the two in the other car barely scratched apart from a cut on the Pole's head. He instinctively thought of survival, his suicide plan having failed, and dragged the girl into the woods. She knew about woods having lived rough in Norfolk, mainly on chocolate and similar food, over Christmas as the man who had kidnapped her raped her time after time, nineteen in all, with a sexual appetite that matched that of a nymphomaniac, experts later said. Into the trees they hurried as ambulances and the police arrived to treat the injured and take them to hospital with the dead baby.

Half an hour later the two, the giant man with blood running into his eyes and the slim, fair-haired girl beside him, arrived at the front door of Cockley Cley Hall, not far from where the body of the headless woman was dumped some years before. Pete rang the door bell and then moved away. When the owner of the hall, Sir Samuel Roberts, the sixth baronet, answered the door, there was no one in sight. Then Pete, who had tried ringing several times before giving up, turned back and lumbered towards Sir Samuel and asked 'Can we come in please?'

The baronet looked at them in amazement. He saw the giant with his left arm hanging loosely, because by that time the shock and pain of the accident had taken over and his left arm had been hurt as well as the slight gash on his forehead. Beside him slim Samantha looking woebegone and bedraggled.

Then Pete said: 'I want to give myself up' and Sir Samuel immediately recognized him as the man whose picture he had seen on television the night before. After his first December victim escaped, a 19-year-old girl whom he raped ten times in hotel rooms where he kept her captive (explaining that he was taking revenge on women because he had been kept for fifteen months on remand in prison awaiting trial on a rape charge for which he was acquitted), police started a hunt for the blue-eyed, fair-haired giant who could charm girls with his shy manner before becoming an insatiable rapist once he had them in his power. They lost him, but after Samantha had vanished and then phoned home on Boxing Day to say she was all right and the phone had gone dead when her frantic parents asked where she was, they linked the two cases and unusually issued a photograph of the giant with the receding hair which was used on television and in all the newspapers.

Sir Samuel invited the couple in, very concerned for the girl. She was wearing a black coat and black boots. Both appeared relaxed although tired and depressed. He at once rang the local policeman and then took the odd couple into the kitchen and made them a cup of tea, while the man tended his wound from a first aid kit that Sir Samuel had provided.

Then he took them into his study because the phone in the kitchen was not working. He made them sit comfortably and gave Samantha the phone. Twice she dialled her parents but could not get through, so Sir Samuel dialled the number.

She said simply 'It's me. It's all over and I'm all right and coming home.' Then: 'I'm at this place in Norfolk but I don't know where I am.' The baronet handed her his card and then she read it out to them. After she had done that Pete the Pole took the phone to speak to Samantha's father. He said 'Hello, it's Pete here. I'm sorry for the trouble what I've given you.'

It was an understatement. The Pole – who never got the chance to finish his cup of tea because the police arrived in force, handcuffed him and took him off – had just ended a seven-year stretch of sex and violent offences which had kept the police very busy, brought terror, fear, humiliation, distress and disgust to a string of victims, and finally death to a baby for no other reason than that the hulking rapist wanted to end his life.

Samantha went home to her parents to resume her life, the Smiths went back to their lonely home to grieve their missing child, and the man who had caused it all was locked up in prison awaiting his trial.

Just who was this man who, like so many others, chose Norfolk as a hiding place for his last crime? How did he change from a normal little boy into a monster who had, it was said at his trial in June, 'the morals of the farmyard'?

He changed after his mother, Hildegard, left home when he was thirteen. His hatred of her was shown when he once spat out her name while attacking one of his victims. He became violent and unruly and developed a hatred for women. His behaviour became such that his father sent him away to school, and while there he played truant and even burnt down the school shed. He had a few jobs after leaving school and eventually joined the Royal Green Jackets with whom he served in Belfast and Berlin, but later left to work on a building site. When he was arrested he served six months in military detention before being discharged in the spring of 1979.

He had several jobs but the one he liked most was being a minicab driver. His hobbies were badminton and body building. It was the latter that was his main passion. He trained and trained with weights and had a superb physique of which he was very proud. This interest kept him going while in jail for rape.

Soon after he came out from his last sentence he met a girl who went to the police alleging that Pete the Pole had kidnapped her, taken her to the West Country and continually raped her at knife point. He had tried to kill her and himself, she claimed, by driving into the path of an oncoming car, but it swerved. She escaped, she said, by hiding in a wardrobe. But after making the statement the girl thought it sounded all so unlikely that she withdrew it. She contacted the police again after the events of Christmas 1986.

After his arrest there were allegations by another woman who had lived with him in south London that he had beaten her up and raped her when she tried to end their affair in 1984.

In August 1985 he was arrested and charged with the rape of a 17-year-old girl. He was in custody for over a year awaiting trial (the fact that he gave to his penultimate victim for wanting revenge on women) but when the case was heard the jury did not believe the victim and found the giant not guilty. Some shook hands with him after he had been released from the dock. They, of course, knew nothing of his previous history, of his violence towards women. They saw him in the way a detective was later to describe him: a shy, bashful young man, a nice chap with good looks and a magnificent body, a superb specimen who attracted the girls who liked his old-fashioned approach. He would ask them out, meet them for a drink – and then he would strike.

After his release Pete the Pole met a dark-haired girl at a badminton club. They became acquaintances and he asked her to meet him for a Christmas drink on 19 December. She went along to meet him and to tell him there was no future in their relationship. He picked her up from her home in his hired car, the one he was to use as a kamikaze vehicle, and they went to Richmond by the River Thames and had a drink. The soft-speaking body-builder plied her with spirits, doubles, suggesting all the time just one more, and she fell asleep in the car on what she thought was the journey home.

Instead she woke in a room in an Epping, Essex, hotel where Peter Chmilowskyj had booked in for two nights as Mr and Mrs Ashmore. He made her undress, said the prosecutor at the trial at St Albans crown court, and 'there followed a weekend of sexual abuse in which he systematically raped her'.

Throughout the two days she was kept naked in the room and she dared not ring her parents because she knew they would be panic-stricken. After two days at Epping the kidnapper took her to Eastbourne. He told the girl, who had not slept for two days: 'I could do away with you and nobody would know.' The girl knew that that was true. In the Eastbourne hotel he tried to stop her breathing after throwing her onto the bed. She tried to talk to him, to reason with him. He told the terrified girl that something in his past had taken him over and he intended to take it out on her. That was the revenge on women he kept referring to, for the time he had to spend on remand before being cleared.

'You're a nice woman but the anger has been building up inside of me' he told her. He made her walk along the beach and told her how easy it would be to throw her in. He made her take a bath and threatened to throw an electric fire in with her which would have electrocuted her.

Then he took her to Bournemouth. The sex attacks went on, but eventually he ran out of money and made the girl go into a bank at Ferndown to draw some out. The cashier recognized her at once and took her behind a security door and slammed it shut so that her captor could do nothing.

He drove off at speed, leaving the girl whom he had raped ten times as she feared for her life to tell the police about her ordeal and give a description they at once recognized. The search for the man and his car – which they were also able to identify – was given top priority, and at 4.00 a.m. on the day before Christmas Eve it was spotted. But the giant rapist, a skilled minicab driver, was off as fast as he could and shook off his police pursuers.

At midnight on Christmas Eve, just as revellers welcomed in Christmas Day, he was parked outside a pub in commuter land in Hertfordshire where Samantha, her boy friend and two other teenagers were ending a lovely evening. They went out to find a cab home, and there was the dark hire car which they mistook for a minicab.

One by one he dropped them off until only Samantha remained in the car, her home the last on the run. The cab drove past her home and then stopped. Pete the Pole changed from the quiet, pleasant cab driver into what he really was. He grabbed the girl by the hair and dragged her across into the front seat. He produced a knife and drove the girl, who was 'in a complete state of terror' the prosecutor said at the trial, to nearby woods where he raped her seven times. Seven times. Just think of it. A happy blonde girl who thought she was being taken home to go to bed and wake the next morning to spend Christmas with her family, and then later with her boy friend, was now in a car being raped time after time by a giant of a man whose face she had never seen before. This great beast was on top of her, threatening to kill her if she resisted. Once. Then twice. Then three times.

This is not what is comfortably called 'domestic rape', where the couple know each other and the rape occurs because the girl says no and the man thinks she means yes and carries on, and later the girl shouts rape. This was a young girl with a total stranger.

Four times. In some houses fathers were being Santa Claus, tiptoeing into the bedroom to put the stockings at the foot of their children's beds. Five, he had raped her a fifth time. Now in some houses the genuine act of love was taking place, husbands and wives, young lovers, celebrating Christmas and happiness and the spirit and joy of the day with pleasure. Six times; the great body-building fanatic with the sex drive of the worst uninhibited animal (who knows no better but is just driven by natural lust) forced himself on the girl again. What was she thinking? Was she on the verge of death with fear or was she becoming numb, frozen with grief and despair and hatred and a feeling of such tremendous terror that her mind was blanking out the great object heaving on top of her like the blackest of clouds? Who can tell, who can repeat feelings like that? Luckily she did not have to go into a witness box to recount in great detail what he had done because he pleaded guilty to eight charges of rape and two of kidnap, specimen charges, just to show the pattern of his activities. He also admitted killing the baby in the car crash, denying murder on the grounds of diminished responsibility, a plea accepted by the prosecution.

Seven times, the seventh rape of Christmas and there was no line to any song of Christmas, just fear, disgust, a desperate longing to get away.

When he had finished he discovered the car was stuck in the mud. She made her only dash for freedom but he caught her, put his arm round her neck and punched her in the face and stomach. 'Don't forget I could kill you now. Try that again and I will kill you' he told her, and she believed the Christmas morning message from this awful man. She did not try again.

In that there was a parallel with the other victim, the 19-year-old. The judge heard that both were bright, intelligent girls, the older girl on her way to university, the younger studying for her A levels, and towards both he 'exhibited what can only be called the morals of the farmyard'. He also did worse. He kept threatening to kill them which, the prosecutor said, made them afraid to escape, creating 'almost in some sort of perverted way, a sort of loyalty'.

It was that which stopped the first girl trying to escape

on the way to Eastbourne, staying with him another night on his promise that he would not touch her, a promise he broke. It was that which prevented Samantha from telling her parents. Fear of death from a man to whom body ravishing was a way of life was a reasonable reaction.

So there on Christmas morning, when she should have been tucked up in bed, was Samantha, ravished, despoiled and petrified. They spent Christmas Day, when she should have been having her turkey and opening her presents, trying to move the car from the mud but failing, and the Pole refreshing himself with rape in between attempts. Four more times. Think of that for Christmas. Eleven times you are raped and hope has gone. Your underclothes have gone too, for this thing you are with is obsessed about dirty shoes and uses your knickers to wipe the mud off his shoes. You are sore and feel dirty inside and out with what has been done to you.

On Christmas evening, when she should have been round the fireside with the family and her boy friend, the rapist dragged her to a stable and found a farmhand to tow the car clear. In the stable (and there was no inn nearby) Samantha could have made the same plea as Mary and asked for shelter and a bed. She was past that moment of courage that would have let her do so. She froze dumb.

The next day, Boxing Day, when she should have been going out with her boy friend and other friends, she was without her coat, sitting waiting for her abductor who was wearing it while he washed all his clothes except his underpants. After that he drove her on to the industrial estate at St Neots, Cambridgeshire, where they had a lunch of Coca Cola and crisps and listened to the radio.

It was the news broadcast they heard that sentenced baby Gemma to death. He knew the police were on to him, and to mark the occasion he raped Samantha four more times. By this time the girl was calmer as he talked about his hatred for his mother. Perhaps there was a gentle side to this monster, perhaps he had feelings for her despite what he was doing, for he had a woman friend with no sex involved, a mother of young children whom he befriended and whose children he played with and cuddled.

But nothing was stopping him on Boxing Day. He had his victim, and her bra hung like a trophy from the driving mirror.

He turned the car towards Norfolk, knowing that it was a great hiding place. He made sure that the girl did not forget her first visit. He raped her four more times on the Saturday, the day after Christmas Eve, as they hid up in the Swaffham area. Samantha was not treated to the delights of hotel rooms like the earlier 19-year-old victim, nor two other women whom he had raped and whom police only learnt about after Samantha's ordeal became public knowledge.

The girl, who came from luxury in Hertfordshire, had to rough it in the car, eating chocolate and drinking soft drinks and putting up with the attentions of the man who wanted revenge on all women. He had now raped her nineteen times. Consider the figure. Nineteen times in four days.

By this time the search for them had reached major proportions. It was 6.50 p.m. Boxing night when her captor allowed Samantha to ring home. Her parents had been waiting, uncomprehending, not knowing what had happened to their daughter, whether she was alive or dead. She would not say where she was but said she would be back at 10.30 p.m. that night. She was not. Of course she was not. He was not going to let her go.

The police talked again to the other girl, the girl who had got away, put two and two firmly together and set out the nationwide call to find Peter Chmilowskyj known as Pete the Pole.

He knew what was going on from the radio. He told his victim that he had done this before, that his victim had escaped and that he did not think he would get away with it again. He drove to the perimeter of the vast Royal Air Force base at Marham on the outskirts of Swaffham, lying off the Downham Market road. It is a bleak, unfriendly area, one sparsely populated and flat, ideal for the bomber base which Marham once was. It was also the station where they used to keep the atomic bombs.

He had decided what he was going to do and told the

girl: he was going to drive into a lorry and she was going to be with him, at his side in death. He raped her to coincide with his announcement and then dictated his suicide note to her. He blamed his parents for what he had become and said: 'I don't know what has happened to me. I can't take any more. What I am doing is the only way out. Goodbye, Pete.' Then the girl wrote her goodbye note: 'To Mum and Dad and everyone. Love you very much. Why did it have to be me? Goodbye.'

He raped the girl twice more. The prosecutor at his trial said 'He made it clear he would kill himself and take the girl with him.' The next morning he drove straight at the Ford Capri and failed in his appalling task, killing an innocent child instead.

Samantha's ordeal had not ended in the death she expected. Imagine sitting beside a man who has told you that you are going to die by driving into another car, sitting there, unable to do anything except leap out to certain death at 80 miles per hour, waiting for death, knowing that it is coming. And then you are alive.

The giant grabbed her and pulled her away from the scene, away from the fresh carnage he had caused and into the woods. But a change came upon him. He muttered as he stumbled: 'I wanted to die, why didn't I die? I wanted to die. I drove head on. Why did we survive?' And for the first time he showed compassion towards the victim whom he had raped so frequently. He told her that he would see that she got home safely. (She did get home safely and went on with her A levels and put it behind her. She, like the other victim, showed great strength of character.)

The man who had horrified the nation pleaded guilty to what he had done and the judge adjourned the case for medical reports. He wanted to know what was the best thing to do: send him to prison or to Broadmoor after Mr Michael Hubbard, QC, had said in the rapist's defence:

'He was a man looking for affection who was triggered into these acts by memories of his appalling childhood. If as a child you had been exposed to beatings such as might be given to an animal, no wonder that lurking in you would be the morals of the farmyard. He had, his whole life, been conditioned to behave as he did. That was never his fault.'

Pete the Pole said much the same in his suicide note: 'Everything that has happened, blame it on my parents, the way they brought me up and treated me.' It was not a view with which his father agreed. He said that his son had lied and cheated and stolen all his life, had broken his heart, brought disgrace on the family and he now washed his hands of him. He went further: he said he should hang. Of course in this liberal country nothing so drastic, so barbaric, happened to a man who could rape all night and bring blood-congealing fear to innocent women.

Five weeks after his trial he appeared before the judge, Mr Justice Phillips, again to hear his fate. He heard his counsel, Mr Hubbard, ask the judge to commit him to Broadmoor with a Restrictive Order which meant that he could not be released just on the opinion of the doctors. It also had to be approved by the Home Secretary of the day, years ahead; and by making such an order the judge would allay public fear, because if no order was made he might be released into the public without their knowledge.

The judge heard from two psychiatrists. One said that the rapist was potentially dangerous, might become the victim of a homosexual attack in prison which could lead to a dangerous situation with his suicidal tendencies. The origin of his problems went back to his childhood and to his liking for alcohol and drugs which had a disturbing effect on his behaviour. The psychiatrist added: 'There is always, in the minds of the public, concern that once treated a person might be released. I would not expect him to be released from Broadmoor by reason of the time it would take to treat the disease.'

It was no soft option. If he spent twenty years in prison he would be released after much the same period of time.

The judge sent him to Broadmoor telling him that his crimes had horrified the nation. He went on:

'I do not propose to catalogue your appalling list of rapes, kidnapping and manslaughter to which you pleaded guilty. Both psychiatrists have agreed you suffered from severe psychopathic disorders and that you present an extreme danger to women though not exclusively. One of the doctors has said that it might lead to homicide in prison.

'No one can say when you will be able to be released into society. My particular concern is to see that the public is safeguarded and to put you in a secure place where there is not the slightest possible chance of you returning to your crimes.'

That is where he is now. The chances of release are virtually nil.

13

Pocock

Raping Swordsman
Who Left Victims for Dead

It was a beautiful July afternoon in 1985, just at the start of the school holidays, when two 13-year-old girls, whom we shall call Jane and Mary, went for a cycle ride in the woods on the back road from Fulbourn near Cambridge over the Gog Magog Hills, and met a modern-day swordsman. He was unlike any knights of old, the Three Musketeers, the Knights of the Round Table, for they acted with perfect manners and chivalry towards ladies of whatever age, particularly pretty teenage young girls. The man with the sword they met was a modern-day rapist with lust in his heart and willing to kill to cover his traces. He wore no shining armour, just the sweatshirt and jeans of a plumber. He was sex-mad, and, like so many chance encounters on summer afternoons, the girls had no idea, never dreamt nor could imagine what was going to happen to them when they cycled in the hills.

The Gog Magog Hills are not big by some standards, though by East Anglian they are enormous, and are a favourite place for walks with the woods, the Roman road that runs straight through to Haverhill and is used for rambling and even an annual running race, and the old Iron Age Wandlebury Ring which has a mystique of its own. So Jane and Mary rode their cycles happily and chattered as girls of that age do.

Suddenly in front of them stepped the man with the sword. It was 30 inches long, an evil blade, and he began swinging it about in front of them; they naturally thought he was playing with them, a man who perhaps had had too much to drink at lunchtime and was fooling about. It did not occur to them at first why a man should have a sword in the heart of the Cambridgeshire countryside. He lunged at them, swished it through the air and, as they made a move to cycle past him, menaced them with it, ordering them to stay where they were.

He told them he was a farmer and they were trespassing on his land. He was a burly man with tattoos on his arms and hands. He was much bigger than them, and what appeared to be a game suddenly became something quite terrifying.

Terror and fear are not confined to the city streets, as we know. Some people believe that the countryside is safe, but nowadays it does not matter where you are if a man is in the mood and is ready to strike and, worse, kill. Two ladies in Hampshire took their dogs for an early afternoon walk on a well-used common and met a madman who slaughtered them. There was nothing about his appearance when he was caught to suggest that he was other than a normal newly-married young man. Another man dragged a little girl from her cycle as she rode for a Saturday morning music lesson. It was a busy road by a canal in a heavily populated area of Hampshire, but no one saw it happen and the killer is still at large. In Devon a 13-year-old girl vanished into thin air in a country lane and, like April Fabb, has never been seen since. Others like Heidi Reddin vanish but are then found.

It was their great misfortune that these two 13-year-olds, Jane and Mary, should run into the man with the sword. Perhaps if they had been there ten minutes before or ten minutes after they might have escaped, for he might have found another victim. It was a haphazard selection, because this 39-year-old man, married twice and with two children by his first wife, a daughter by his second, was sex-mad. He thought and talked of nothing else, and at the slightest opportunity had sex. He told workmates that he often had sex several times a day with different partners and if, while out on his rounds as a plumber, he was able to give a girl a lift he would do his utmost to persuade her to have sex, and apparently often succeeded.

Why he chose this spot to rape this summer afternoon as the birds sang and the rabbits played in the hedgerow, and gliders soared above from the nearby former wartime RAF Battle of Britain station at Duxford, no one but he knows. But there they were, this group of three, two terrified girls and a man wielding power with his sword.

He ordered the girls off their bikes and into the trees. He ordered them to remove their underwear, and, when they had done that – at swordpoint and the shining blade, so sharp and evil looking, glistened in the sunlight – he forced their pants into their mouths as gags and then tied their hands behind their backs.

He left them for a moment but they did not have time or, I suppose, the inclination to try to escape. They were mesmerized with terror at that point and by the time they realized their predicament (because they were both intelligent and alert girls) it was too late.

He came back and made them walk to his car, an old, rusting Volvo. They took note of it as he forced them onto the back seat. They also noticed that he had a tattoo on one arm, a green and blue heart with the names of his sons, and the word 'love' tattooed across the fingers of one hand. He made them lie down on the back seat and put a blanket over them, then got into the driver's seat. He started the engine and drove down the hill and turned east.

He drove 50 miles to Bartlow, a small Cambridgeshire village near the Suffolk border. He ordered the girls out and marched them at blade point into thick undergrowth. When he asked how old they were they said they were ten, hoping that this would stop him. They were astute and both suspected exactly what fate lay in store for them. The man did not care. His lust was overpowering him like a volcanic explosion. Nothing was going to stop him. They were his captives and he was going to have his way with them. He showed the petrified girls some pornographic pictures and then got on with the business. He told them to strip and, when they had done so, now doing everything he told them, this horror with a sword, he had his way.

First he assaulted Jane and then he raped Mary. When he had finished he allowed the girls to dress. It is almost impossible to imagine how they felt. They had been cycling through the countryside one minute, nice ordinary schoolgirls, and an hour later this terrible man had deflowered them, one in a way that showed his total contempt for women. This was a 13-year-old virgin he had raped; another 13-year-old he had indecently assaulted while she was naked.

They barely knew where they were, but once they were dressed he promised to take them back to their cycles. The feeling of relief that he was to do nothing more must have been immense. But it was a lie. He drove away from the spot and headed off who knows where, for he drove and drove on an erratic course for 100 miles and ended up where so many like him have ended before at the end of their trail to cover their crime: Norfolk.

For this foul deed he chose Emily's Wood at Weeting, forest land not far into the county but an ideal wood in which to finish off these girls on whom he had lusted but who knew too much. He had not attempted to disguise himself. He had spoken to them and they knew his description, his voice, his car and his manner. He knew they were bright girls by the way they had tried to stop him doing what he wanted by saying they were ten years old. They were smart and they could put him behind bars for a very long time. They had to be silenced.

First he took Jane into the wood, clutching his sword. There was to be no mercy. He drove the blade, the thin 30 inch blade, straight through her body. It penetrated the lower tip of her left lung and went into her heart. As he did so, she screamed, and her friend Mary heard the scream of a girl whose heart had just been stabbed by a man bent on murder to silence his victim so she would never be able to give evidence against him, never be able to tell of the wicked things he had done.

He covered the body and went back for her friend. He picked her up, the girl weeping with fear, and put a coat over her head. She believed with excellent cause that she was being carried to her death. When they reached her friend the coat slipped off Mary and to her horror she saw her friend lying apparently dead and she knew her turn was coming any second.

The man with the sword stood over her and then thrust hard and accurately, pinning her to the ground as the sharp blade slid through her slim young body. Her jugular vein was severed as the blade passed between her gullet and windpipe. The man also inflicted other wounds to her chest and abdomen.

Jane stirred, so he had one final slash at her – what he supposed to be the clinching death blow.

He certainly left them believing them to be dead; but he was wrong. As he washed the blood off the sword on his way home to the Newmarket area, using a river just over the border into Suffolk not far from where the body of Leoni Williams, aged three, was to be recovered, Mary stirred. She had expected death but had done everything in her power to avoid it. She had held her breath and pretended to be dead after the man had pinned her to the ground like a butterfly. It was her salvation.

When she realized he had gone she struggled to her feet. She did not want to. With her terrible wounds she wanted to stay where she was and rest. It would have meant death if she had done so. She and Jane would have lain there and gradually slipped into unconsciousness and died. Not many people went to the area. It would have been luck to have been found.

But she forced herself up and found a piece of wood which she broke in two to make a crutch. She roused Jane and the two girls forced themselves to move, oh so slowly with their awful injuries, to the road over 100 yards away to stop a passing motorist. He drove them to the police and, at the police station, as they waited for the ambulance, as they passed in and out of consciousness, the two very brave teenagers were able to give sufficient detail for the police to start the hunt for the man who had done such a wicked deed.

Mary was able to tell them about the car and about the tattoos. It was just what the police needed. A woman detective immediately recognized the details of the tattoos, the green and blue heart with two boys' names on it. Within thirty-six hours the police had arrested Terence Pocock, aged thirty-nine, a self-employed heating engineer who had worked as a plumber. He had a long history of indecent assault, robbery with violence and theft. His second wife knew of his taste for girls, and never allowed him out on his own socially, neighbours said.

He was tried at Norwich in December 1985. He pleaded guilty to six charges: two of attempting to murder the girls, two of kidnapping them, one of raping Mary and one of indecently assaulting Jane. It did not take long to hear the case.

Mr David Stokes, prosecuting, told the story of how the girls were stopped by Pocock with his sword and how he took them first to Bartlow for the rape and indecent assault and then on to Emily's Wood in Norfolk for the bid to murder them. The prosecutor told how Pocock took Jane into the wood and thrust the sword into her heart. Mr Stokes said: 'It was an accurate blow and meant to kill.' Having done it he covered the girl, who was in agony but amazingly alive, with a body warmer.

Then Pocock went back for Mary, who saw her friend when the coat Pocock had draped over her slipped off. The prosecutor said: 'Then suddenly she felt the sword going right through her and sticking in the ground. Her jugular vein was severed when the weapon passed through her gullet and windpipe. Pocock inflicted other stab wounds into her chest and abdomen.'

Later Pocock told the police: 'As I stabbed one girl, the other started to move, so I chopped her across the head and stabbed her in the throat.' And he explained why he did it. 'I did it because there would be no repercussion. They wouldn't be able to give evidence against me.'

There was no doubt that this was what was in his mind. He admitted it when the time came, and the girls did not have to give evidence about the appalling things he had done to them. It was something in his favour. There was not much else that could be said that put him in any other kind of light than bad.

The prosecutor continued with his sad story. He said that despite the murderous attack Mary stayed calm and cool and played dead by holding her breath. He said: 'She behaved with tremendous courage and presence of mind. She wanted to go to sleep and there is little doubt that if she had done so neither of them would have survived.'

It is speculation in hindsight, but the police would have been in difficulty if they had died. They were miles from home, their cycles would have been found in the wood on the Gog Magog Hills, and there were no witnesses to what had happened that caused them to travel so far and with whom. There might have been a witness at Bartlow but none came forward. The pathologist would have found that the girls had been murdered with a sword but there would have been no weapon at the scene, no marks to show what kind of car had been there. The police would have gone round all known sex attackers in the surrounding counties and would inevitably have questioned Pocock. He might have cracked under questioning, but there was nothing to show that he had remorse for what he had done, certainly not until he knew the evidence against him from the girls. But if he had not confessed, that might have left the police with an unsolved crime on their hands.

The courage of the girls made absolutely sure this was not the case. For, said the prosecutor, instead of going to sleep Mary managed to make a crutch and the two staggered the long 100 yards to the road where passing motorist Peter Hullett played the Good Samaritan; because of his prompt action and that of the hospital staff the girls lived.

Consultant surgeon, Mr Michael O'Brien, told the judge, Mr Justice Staughton, that both the girls were lucky to be alive. Under any normal rules Jane should have been dead after the blade pierced her heart. One of the blows had cut her ear in two. She spent five days on a life support machine but came out alive although, the surgeon points out, she, like Mary, 'will be scarred for life and the psychological effects of these horrific injuries are incalculable.'

What was there to say about Pocock who sat heavily in the dock and listened to everything that was being said about him and what he had done? Not very much really. A psychiatrist who interviewed him said his behaviour was calculated, cool and callous and he could find no sign of guilt or remorse or self-recrimination. Pocock's defending counsel, Mr Adrian Whitfield, said, 'There is no evidence of psychiatric problems.'

That was, as is often the case, the trouble. What makes a man with an eye for the girls suddenly behave in that way? Who carries a sword about on the off chance that he will meet a girl or two, have his way with them and then drive the sword through them as though on a medieval battlefield? Drive the sword through them to pin them to the ground like a butterfly on a board? Who expects the plumber to be a man like that? Rapist, perhaps, but very unlikely; thief, perhaps, and it has happened I suppose. But for a plumber to be carrying a sword on a beautiful summer's day in the heart of Cambridgeshire, with the intent of finding a girl to rape and then kill to make sure she did not tell, is pushing belief to its boundaries.

The judge did not mince words with Pocock. He jailed him for life five times and told him:

'These offences constituted as serious an attack as I have ever heard. Your responsibility is scarcely any less than if you have succeeded in killing one or both of these girls as you nearly did. You thought only of yourself, trying to kill these girls because you didn't want them to give evidence.'

He said that there was some evidence that Pocock showed remorse but only after he had been arrested and knew the evidence against him.

After Pocock had been taken to the cells to start his sentences, knowing that throughout the long years he would always be in danger of attack from other prisoners, who have their own code when it comes to child attackers, the judge praised the motorist for being a Good Samaritan and the hospital staff for saving the girls' lives.

He also had a good word for the police. He said: 'In the past police have sometimes been criticized when they fail to apprehend a rapist for some time. It seems to me that their job was very well done on this occasion.'

And after the case was over, and everyone was leaving, the then head of Norfolk CID, Detective Chief Superintendent Maurice Morson, praised the courage of the girls, both of whom were by then back at school and making excellent progress after their ordeal. He said that their courage, fortitude and commonsense were the main reasons why Pocock was caught and convicted. He went on: 'These girls have our admiration and appreciation. They gave us vital, crucial information and without such help we wouldn't have made an early arrest.' He said the police were very impressed by the way the girls had behaved, their sensible attitude and what they had remembered during their terrifying ordeal, one of the most horrifying sequences of events they had ever investigated.

It was just as well they had. It saved their lives, caught the man who had terrorized them, and took them back into the family background that created such sense.

14

Kempton

Mourner Killed and Dumped

Fair-haired Jeanette Kempton was a divorcee, aged thirty-one, who lived in Brixton and had a slightly bizarre way of life – living with her ex-husband and having boy friends in that area of south London. She enjoyed a drink and was happy and popular.

How she ended up in the dumping fields of East Anglia and on the slab of a Norfolk seaside town mortuary is a mystery that, like so many, has no solution.

It may be that she was taken and thrown in a ditch on the Norfolk–Suffolk border on the Earl of Strabroke's estate near Wangford, just into Suffolk, after she had been hit on the head and then manually strangled. It may be that she had picked up someone in south London and then gone away for a few days and the man who took her and enjoyed sex then decided to kill her. This seems unlikely for Brixton to the depths of Norfolk and Suffolk is a long way and involves a torturous route out of London. Much more likely is that she was killed on her home patch and then driven out to the country, where she was thrown into a ditch near a bridleway. This meant that the killer had to turn off the main road, then onto a side road and then onto the bridleway which runs between two maize fields and is well used by walkers and people out shooting. It was two men returning from a day's shoot who spotted the body and called the police, who found it was decomposed and had been there for several days.

Within a few days they knew who she was, where she had come from, what she had been doing, but had no idea why she was killed or why she was found where she was in mid-February 1989.

She had last been seen walking with considerable difficulty (because she was drunk) away from the Loughborough Arms in Brixton on the evening of 2 February. She had been having a drinking session with her boy friend Barry, and he left her to go home to his wife in Mitcham, Surrey. A witness at the inquest in December said she saw Barry, who had a false hand, and Jeanette in a car; but Barry denied this.

When she tottered off, full of five and a half pints or the equivalent of eleven shorts, she was clutching a wreath to take to a friend's funeral the next day. She did not turn up and the wreath has never been seen again.

She was wearing a maroon coat and black high-heeled shoes, a gold bracelet and two rings and was carrying her purse. All these were missing when she was found in that unfriendly ditch many miles away from home. Some items of clothing were missing, too, suggesting she had had sex before she was killed.

When her body was found and the inquest in Norfolk carried out, Suffolk police started inquiries because the body was on their patch. The same situation had existed when Linda Smith's body was found at Polstead some twenty-eight years before. She was a 12-year-old girl from Earls Colne, in Essex who had been abducted from the roadside and taken away to be strangled and dumped by the Red Barn (where Maria Marten was murdered by William Corder). The county in which the body is found does the investigation, irrespective of where the crime is committed.

The Kempton inquiry was exceptionally thorough. Police took 400 statements and interviewed 3,500 people, but the sum of the inquiries was nil. They used the HOLMES system, the Home Office Large Major Enquiries System, a computer that sifts statements and evidence, linking, rejecting, matching up, comparing notes electronically.

HOLMES, like the detective of that name, is wonderful for quickly turning up the obvious which the normal human eventually finds. Unfortunately in this case it turned up nothing.

The murder was featured on *Crimewatch*, the BBC 1 monthly crime programme which is watched by millions of viewers and which has a high success rate in finding new evidence from a public who are only too willing to help. But with the Kempton murder the response was poor. Only forty people contacted the police and the result was again of no help at all.

Every detail the police possessed and were prepared to make public was shown. There was the dark blue or green Transit-type van with a high roof seen in the Wangford area on 5 February. The person who saw it thought it was a rental van with 'hire' written on it and with a London phone number starting 01 but no other figures. It has never been traced.

Then there was a white Japanese-make car seen in the area, with a woman answering Jeanette's description in the passenger seat on 6 February, four days after she left the Brixton pub. That has never been traced either.

Her body was found on 18 February. Her knickers and tights were missing. So too was the distinctive wreath of red and white flowers.

When the inquest was held on 30 November, one new interesting fact emerged: she had been hit on the head with a blunt instrument forty-eight hours before her death, which was caused by manual strangulation. But when that actually happened and where was not known. Nor was it known how Jeanette Kempton, mother of two, managed to travel to East Anglia and whether she was alive or dead.

The verdict was unlawful killing and the coroner said he hoped more evidence might come to light. It has not. It is another in the long list of people who walk out of a building, whether it be house or pub or club or restaurant, and vanish.

Her family are lucky in the sad sense that she was found and her body buried, for many, like the Fabbs and the Newings and the Exalls, never have that peace of mind.

15

Davidson

Defrocked Rector Killed by Lion

On the edge of the salt marshes and just a little inland, lying between Wells-Next-The-Sea and Blakeney Point and its bird sanctuary, is the village of Stiffkey. It was mentioned in the Domesday Book and has a very old church, St John the Baptist. It is famous for several things: its cockles, its brick and flint houses, how you pronounce its name (for some say it Stiffkey and others Stewkey), and its Hall, built by the Bacon family in 1578, little of which now remains.

It is an interesting but not unusual Norfolk village and would have stayed that way but for one man, the Rev. Harold Davidson, the rector from 1906 to 1932.

He lived in the twenty-room rectory by the A149, which runs round the Norfolk coast from King's Lynn via Hunstanton and Cromer to Great Yarmouth, with his wife Molly. Theirs was a quarrelsome marriage with a suggestion that the fourth of their children born during the First World War was not his. He obtained the living through his connection with the Townshend family and it was expected that he would be a normal country parson tending his flock of not that many souls.

He was not. He brought to that little village that straggles the roadside, and where hardly anyone ever stopped, a notoriety that was almost unequalled in ecclesiastical history.

Harold Davidson, born in Southampton in 1875, educated at Whitgift School, and Exeter College, Oxford, entertainer whose roles included 'Charley's Aunt', assistant chaplain to the Household Cavalry at Windsor, and wartime naval chaplain, was one of the very few Church of England clergymen to be defrocked for immoral behaviour and certainly the first to be eaten by a lion.

Davidson was in fact two people in one. One was a dedicated priest whose real parish was not in the deep rural countryside but on the streets of Soho, where he was known as the 'Prostitute's Padre', a title he proudly proclaimed, who returned to his Norfolk people at the weekend to take the services and see to their needs before rushing back to London on the first train on Monday morning. The other was an impish, foolish man who chatted up young girls on the streets, in cafés with the Nippies (the name for the waitresses in the Lyons Corner Houses – his favourite type of girl), and in bedrooms. He did extremely stupid acts but always insisted that he had never tried and most certainly did not have sex with any of the girls. He took some to Paris where he had a friend who ran a school for girls to learn domestic service.

He was an eccentric, renowned around Soho as a man who ran everywhere; a fearless tiger just 5 feet 3 inches tall who would tackle even the largest pimp; a man who had sixteen pockets in his suit, packed with letters and notes but very little money because he was always short and in trouble and had even been bankrupt. Some thought he did good works but many of the girls he tried to save or chat up thought he was a nuisance.

He was litigious, and throughout his life, and particularly after he was kicked out of the Church in a ceremony at Norwich Cathedral (for which he was typically late) on 21 October 1932, he protested his innocence right until the end of his life.

It was also part of his eccentricity that he needed very little sleep – a nap in a chair and he was up and literally running again. He did good works and drove some people to fury, but even now, over fifty years on, it is difficult to be certain whether he was a dirty old man, a meddling old fool or a very genuine man who was totally misjudged by those who tried him and condemned him.

His activities were such that they were very well known from the early twenties when he started his weird lifestyle, leaving Stiffkey on the first train on Monday morning and making it back to the church on time on the following Sunday morning, often pedalling furiously through the lanes in his cassock in a race against time (he missed funerals), after catching the last train from Liverpool Street on Saturday night.

He took to this way of life because his wife had been unfaithful to him during the war. Instead of staying in Norfolk, he brought his new parishioners, the city girls, some of whom knew all about sex, to the country occasionally to the delight of the local lads, for working in the rectory kitchen or garden soon palled and they strayed into the paths and byways. The rectory was always full, the sound of laughter and raised voices crashing through the flintstone walls or carrying across the fields from the garden.

There were many girls that he helped, aged fourteen to twenty, but three were to provide his downfall and lead him before the consistory court in Church House, Lambeth, in 1932 to face charges of immorality under the Clergy Discipline Act, 1892. The first was Rose Ellis, a 20-year-old prostitute whom he met when she was down on her luck and who caught his eye. She was the kind of girl the Actors' Church Union (of which the rector was a very active member, saving girls) looked after. It was a friendship in which the rector played the father figure, the kindly uncle and the legal guardian, and it lasted ten years or so. She did not give evidence at the trial, but it was to her the private eye employed by the Bishop of Norwich's advisers went and it was she, aided by a drink or two or more, who told all after a parishioner had reported his rector, not just for immorality but for slackness. The complainant, a major, did not like the rector hurtling through the country lanes on his cycle, surplice billowing in the wind, late for service, only to find the congregation had gone; failing to take Remembrance Day war memorial service; the parties at the rectory with the London girls taking to the hay fields with the local lads. He wrote to the bishop, alleging immorality under the Act; but that Act had sweeping meanings when it came to immorality. It included drunkenness, idling, gambling, swearing and other wickednesses including adultery.

The second girl was Barbara Harris, who was to accuse him of the five charges he faced and denied: systematically misbehaving himself with young women. He met her outside Marble Arch tube station when she was sixteen, and his approach was the old one used by many men to introduce themselves. He tipped his hat and asked 'Excuse me, Miss, but has anyone told you how much you look like Mary Brian, the movie actress?' She went with him to Lyons and he told her how he could get her into pictures (not true, said the rector). He often visited her in her room and Barbara, experienced with men since she was seduced at the age of fifteen, said he was always after her, trying to have sex, trying to rape her and wanted to marry her – all accusations that the tiny rector strongly denied.

The third girl was Estelle, the 15-year-old daughter of an actress friend of Davidson's, who had stated publicly before the trial that she had often left her daughter in his charge while she was at the theatre and was happy to do so. It was that girl, fifteen and attractive, who was to prove the case against him.

After the complaint, the bishop, Dr Pollock, contacted his legal advisers and it was they who hired the private detective agency who got a statement from Rose Ellis, who immediately repented and regretted what she had said and withdrew her statement. Too late: the statement was part of what the ecclesiastical authorities needed. They did not want to take the case to court but hoped that Davidson would resign his living and the whole matter could be hushed up.

They did not know the rector. He was a fighter and he was not going to go down without a struggle, particularly as he insisted, and did until his death, that it was all lies. He used all his skills as a show business and clerical performer to make his case the front page news throughout the summer of 1932 and then big news until his death seven years later. The bishop was still dithering about what to do when Davidson pre-empted him. He told the *Evening News* in London, thereby breaking the story, that he would fight to the bitter end.

In the run-up to the trial, switched from Norwich (where it should have been held) to London to accommodate all the interested parties and the witnesses (the rector planned to call nearly 500, but in the event did not), there was tremendous publicity. This was the age of no television and very little radio and so the papers were the source of all news, and a case like this, as it would be now, was lapped up by the eager public. It had everything: sex, a vicar, Paris, more sex, prostitutes, important people, more sex, eccentrics, different venues and a certain amount of humour.

Rose Ellis told one paper how she was bribed; the rector sold his life story; his actress friend told how she had known him for twenty years without a bad word spoken about him, and then two papers now defunct, the *Daily Herald* and *Empire News*, were fined for contempt of court, a crime they did not know existed so rarely are consistory courts held.

Just before the trial two things happened which affected the story: the rector preached to packed congregations which overspilled outside the church, and Barbara Harris sat down in her bedsit and wrote seven pages to the Bishop of Norwich which set out the case that she would tell as a witness to end the rector's career.

No one knew quite what to expect when it finally started, just how the Rev. Harold Davidson would face his accusers on 29 March 1932. If they thought it was going to be low key they were much mistaken, for he arrived with his crowd of admirers, including some ladies from Stiffkey. He held a cardboard suitcase which he held aloft like the chancellor on Budget Day, and waved a large cigar. The other Davidson was in his element.

The chancellor who was in charge of proceedings was the chancellor of the diocese of Norwich, the Worshipful F. Keppel North, who was also chairman of Norfolk Quarter Sessions which dealt with normal criminals. He kept all in order, particularly when the other Davidson, the one full of mischief and silliness, took over.

Public attitudes towards morals and behaviour in those days are so far removed from today that it is difficult to imagine how it was. Sex was never described as such, different words being used that did not give a hint of what was going on. The public were kept in ignorance, whether because those who edited the papers thought that censorship was the right thing to do or because they were genuinely prudish and thought they shared the public belief and assumed they did not want to know. Some of the things that were given in evidence (and by today's standards they were very little) were either written round in such a way as to appear meaningless or not mentioned at all.

Davidson faced five charges and when Roland Oliver, QC, representing the bishop, opened the case he said that 'you see sex running through the whole thing'. The charges meant that the rector had systematically been misbehaving himself for years with young women, and that meant from fifteen upwards.

Sex may have been about but in fact the string of witnesses (with the exception of Barbara) told not of sex but of a little man pestering them and making himself a thorough nuisance. He was always around the cafés, chatting up Nippies, flattering them about their looks, their teeth (he had a great interest in teeth and would study them like a vet with a horse) holding their hands, looking into their eyes, giving them pecks as kisses and generally irritating many but pleasing some. There was nothing more than that: no romps in beds or the hay of Norfolk. Just a clergyman who sometimes wore a dog collar and more often did not, who was always around, helping girls in distress and annoying others who were not and were just doing a day's work.

Barbara Harris was different. She had been seduced at fifteen and was experienced when Davidson first met her, attracted by her eyes and her wriggle as she walked, a wriggle practised to attract attention, hopefully, of a film director, for she was a tremendous film fan and Davidson had only to say that she looked like Garbo for her to come to life. His aim was to improve her life, get her to work and take her away from the slippery slope into prostitution that he saw ahead for her. He paid her rent from time to time, got her jobs, encouraged her.

But that was not all. Barbara said that he was always kissing her, was naked in her room, tried to rape her, tried to have sex with her all the time, in fact kept on and on about it and even said he would commit suicide if she did not allow him to go to bed with her on one occasion. She accused him of often being in her room wearing just the top of her pyjamas and claiming he said he wanted to marry her. Once, to cool his ardour, she had given him a black eye.

It was a long litany suggesting improper and immoral behaviour over a long period of time, and, if she was right, the rector was desperately in love with her and his infatuation drove him to perform in the way she described at great length.

The court tried to imagine the diminutive priest naked and climbing into bed with this attractive girl, regularly trying to bed her, regularly in her room, even when boy friends were with her. It was a possible picture. For this was a man to whom all things seemed possible. He was sometimes back stage amongst scantily dressed girls doing good works for the Lord – and he was very proud of his nickname of 'Prostitute's Padre' given him by the girls he tried to help (he claimed that he had given advice to 500 out of the 2,000 he had picked up over the years) whom he met in the streets.

Towards the end of her evidence, which lasted nearly ten hours, the court heard that Barbara had been kept in lodgings and food by the bishop's advisers during the time she wrote the letter and appeared as a witness. It was, said the rector's counsel, 'a monstrous and improper thing to have done'.

It was the second prong of what the rector called the dirty trick department by the bishop's team, because they had also employed the private eye who paid Rose Ellis forty shillings, which caused Davidson to write to the bishop and say 'You are ten up on Judas – he only got thirty pieces of silver.' He also wrote to him to say 'The ecclesiastical mind has been guilty in the past history of some very underhand methods but has never stooped so low.'

When it came to Davidson's turn he naturally denied any impropriety whatsoever. Barbara's story was not true, he affirmed, wriggling and moving about on his chair because he was incapable of sitting still. It was her soul he was after not her body.

He was a surprising man, switching from serious to silly, telling the court, for instance, that although he had been a naval chaplain in the war (and had been caught in a raid on a brothel when trying to root out a prostitute who was giving VD to the seamen) he did not know what a buttock was! He insisted – and in truth there was no one really to contradict him except Barbara, whose testimony was exactly the opposite, and Rose, who was not called because everyone thought she would be unreliable (and that added to Davidson's downfall because she might have supported him) – that he was a misunderstood and innocent man whose only interest was saving souls for Christ amongst those unfortunate women he met as he padded the streets night and day for years around the West End and Soho. There was no immorality, no adultery and no importuning, he insisted and kept on insisting until the end of his days.

It was sincere even though slightly eccentric evidence from the man accused of immorality, and all might have been well but for one final piece of evidence the prosecution produced.

Mr Roland Oliver handed him a photograph which had been taken on Easter Monday, 28 March, the day before the trial began. Two months later in May when he was giving his evidence, it was in his hand, possibly for the first time, possibly not. But on the day before he was on trial for his job and life Davidson had pushed his self-destructor button with a vengeance.

The picture was of a dark-haired girl, well developed; and there, adjusting her shawl so that it did not fall off, was the rector. The picture was taken by two Fleet Street freelance photographers and the rector said that he was doing the girl's mother, the actress Mae, a favour because she wanted to go on the stage and needed a good photograph. Originally they had all gone up to Stiffkey to do photographs on Palm Sunday but the photographer ran out of plates for the swimsuit snaps after taking many of girls in pyjamas.

The picture that Davidson studied was of a girl who probably had nothing else on (the view of the chancellor) and whose left shoulder was bare. There was one more thing that was terribly wrong: the girl was only fifteen. The rector studied it and then Mr Oliver leant forward and, in a supreme theatrical and courtroom gesture, handed the shaken priest another photograph. It stopped him from speaking, such was the effect.

The photograph showed the rector, looking glazed, with his left hand still clutching a small part of the shawl on the girl's left shoulder; but the rest of the shawl had fallen away to expose not just her naked back but her naked buttocks and legs. The rector's hand held the shawl on her left buttock. He was fully dressed.

The effect on the court was dramatic. The chancellor told Davidson to keep his distance when he moved towards him, apparently disgusted. Everyone was astonished. The rector tried to explain. It was an accident, he said, the shawl had slipped from his hand, it was a set-up job, a trap, no money involved, would never have done such a thing, an accident, he did not know. They had definitely not been taken for publication either in Britain or abroad. He thought she was wearing a bathing costume under the shawl and had no idea that she had hardly anything on.

At one stage the rector said: 'Anyone who was consciously a party to a photograph of that sort ought to be put in prison.' Mr Oliver agreed. He added 'No one would blame the child.' Davidson nodded. 'Nor the poor fool of a parson who was trapped into it.'

The final speeches were made and the long trial ended on 6 June, although there had been several breaks for the chancellor to decide on his verdict. He had much to think about but the whole matter really revolved round the one

question: Did he believe the rector or did he believe
Barbara Harris? He believed Barbara and said so when he
pronounced judgement on 8 July 1932. Davidson,
inevitably, was late.

He had not been idle during the time that elapsed
between the end of the trial and the verdict. His name
appeared regularly in the papers, particularly when he
wrestled with the man deputed to take his place at Stiffkey
over the Bible on the lectern in front of a packed
congregation which overspilled out on to the graveyard.
Women shouted and clapped and Davidson pleaded for
order before he could preach his sermon on the text
'Blessed are the pure in heart, for they shall see God.'

It was inevitable that the rector should be late for his
judgement day. He carried a silk top hat and was dressed
in clerical black. He sat still for once to listen to the
chancellor. The Rev. Harold Davidson, who had a living
worth £800 a year (a lot of money in those days), who was
a partner and school friend of Maundy Gregory of the
Lloyd George Honours scandal, needed to, because the
chancellor did not mince words. He said:

'I watched Mr Davidson anxiously for something like
four days in the witness box and I do not believe him. His
evidence in chief was a tissue of falsehoods. He went
down an absolutely discredited witness on whose oath no
reliance can be placed.'

The chancellor went on in like vein and then said: 'I
cannot accept his evidence where it is in conflict with
anyone else's evidence.' He was, said the chancellor, 'an
awful liar' – damning stuff, particularly as he was talking
about a man of the cloth.

It was not just that which condemned the little rector.
His failure to call Rose Ellis, who was available but
considered by everyone else as unreliable, also helped
convict him. But the vital testimony was that of Barbara
Harris and, as Chancellor North said, if she was not
speaking the truth that was the end of the matter. But he
said 'I have come to a definite conclusion. I believe
Barbara.' He therefore found Davidson guilty on five
charges. The rector shot from his seat and hurried down

the Great Hall and out into the crowd.

It was over three months before the Bell, Book and Candle ceremony in Norwich Cathedral, and Davidson kept the fight going all those weeks and even after all hope seemed to have gone.

A few days after the verdict he discovered one of his churches had been locked against him, even as *The Church Times* blasted those who tried him.

Then the rector went back to the stage again, appearing before a packed house at Wimbledon to raise money for his appeal and save him borrowing from his friends.

At the end of the month he was refused leave to appeal against the findings of the chancellor on the facts against him by the Judicial Committee of the Privy Council sitting with three bishops as assessors.

By August the Bishop of Norwich had acted and barred him from his church in Stiffkey. He held a farewell service, which was packed, and afterwards went to see the major who had accused him but Davidson received a kick up the backside for his pains.

Eight days before sentence was due to be passed, Davidson made one more legal appeal, this time to the Judicial Committee of the Privy Council on the grounds that the chancellor had got the law wrong. Davidson was out of funds and had to appear himself.

On the day he was to be thrown out everyone was present except – as was almost certain to be the case – the rector. He sent a telegram from Newmarket to say he had been slightly delayed. But as the telegram was read there were great cheers outside the cathedral as he arrived and he ran in with his silk top hat. As the Bishop was about to pronounce sentence the rector asked for the right to speak, which was granted, and he started by saying that he was entirely innocent in the sight of God. It only held up the inevitable.

For the rest of his life, five years, Davidson did everything he could to show that he was innocent. He humiliated himself to raise the money to keep his appeal against the findings alive, to get the Archbishop of Canterbury and the Bishop of Norwich to restore him to his living, insisting all the time that he was innocent.

He told the people who crowded the Golden Mile at the Lancashire seaside resort of Blackpool of his case as he stood in a barrel on the front, replacing a starving woman as one of the top exhibits that summer. Tens of thousands flocked to see him, and he was really in trouble with the authorities because in 1935 he was charged with starving himself in a public place with intent to commit suicide. Suicide and death were the last things he wanted. He wanted to be alive to get his job back. He was found not guilty and sued the corporation, receiving damages of nearly £400.

He was always in trouble with the Blackpool council, being fined regularly for causing a breach of the peace and even obstructing the footpath. But the only time he went to prison was when his last London landlady caught up with him, and he spent nine days in Walton Jail in Liverpool for non-payment of rent.

Eventually the Blackpool crowds tired of him and he moved on to Skegness after three years to open for the 1937 summer season as a modern Daniel in the lion's den. It was all part of keeping his name in the public limelight, sueing anyone who said anything that he considered libellous about him, and libelling the ecclesiastical authorities as much as he could to make them sue him so that his case could be aired in court again. They were never so unwise as to do so.

So there he was in the den after giving the crowd his views about his case, blasting the Church authorities but not the Church itself, for he did not blame the Church of England, only the leaders.

It was the evening of 28 July 1937 and the man who usually went into the den with the ex-rector was on his night off. He was to say at the inquest later that the lions, Freddie and Toto, were docile, his own 8-year-old daughter often went into the cage, and customers did so too to pat them.

No one went into the 112 square foot cage with the rector for his two or three minute chat with the lions. What happened was described to the inquest by a

16-year-old girl called Irene who was employed as a part-time lion-tamer and was standing by the cage as Davidson, who was remarkably brave as he did not like animals, entered.

She said: 'When he went in the lion Freddie was in the way and he tried to slip between him and the back of the cage. He was nowhere near the lioness and I am sure he did not touch her. When Mr Davidson tried to get out of the way Freddie reared up on his haunches to get him with his front paws.

'I got into the cage and tried to beat the lion off but it dragged Mr Davidson to a corner near the other locked gate and we could not move him until Freddie dropped him. The lioness was still at the other end of the cage.'

Freddie had dragged Davidson round the cage like a cat with a mouse. The giant jaws broke a bone in his neck and caused terrible lacerations to his face. He died two days later in a diabetic coma.

The verdict at the inquest, where the assistant lion-tamer told how she went in to face the lion, was misadventure.

It was a reasonable summing-up of his life. It was a long adventure that became a misadventure. He was a character, an eccentric in an age when there were still many about. Nowadays he would have his fifteen minutes of glory, perhaps even longer, but the time has long gone and the appetite, viciously sharpened, of a much larger public is for change and fresh characters weekly, if not daily. A man like Davidson would be far too complex, far too quicksilver for today's poorly-educated public. He would need time to put his case and TV shows do not have time.

He was buried in Stiffkey churchyard and for years pilgrimages have been made there by ladies who remember him with affection and delight.

He may have been genuine, he may not have been. He certainly did good and probably very little harm. He bubbled with life and gave a great deal of amusement and enjoyment and thought, too, to many people. It is not a bad epitaph.

Index